10-

18/111

2

D0130856

Porch Stories

Porch
Stories

A Grandmother's

Guide to Happiness

Jewell Parker Rhodes

ATRIA BOOKS

New York   London   Toronto   Sydney

ATRIA BOOKS

1230 Avenue of the Americas
New York, NY 10020

ISBN-13: 978-0-7434-9711-4
ISBN-10:   0-7434-9711-2

First Atria Books hardcover edition September 2006

1   3   5   7   9   10   8   6   4   2

ATRIA BOOKS is a trademark of Simon & Schuster, Inc.

Designed by Jaime Putorti

Line art by Gilbert Fletcher

Manufactured in the United States of America

For information regarding special discounts for bulk purchases,
please contact Simon & Schuster Special Sales at 1-800-456-6798
or business@simonandschuster.com.

To Grandmother Ernestine,

who raised me, infused me with life, and taught me the power of

stories. More than thirty years a spirit, you are in my thoughts

each and every day. I love you very, very much.

Acknowledgments

I would like to acknowledge and thank grandmothers everywhere and all women who served as a wise elder for a daughter, a grandchild, a sister, or friend when she needed it most.

Porch Stories

"Jewell, child. Wear clean underwear.
Always. Don't let folks think you're trash.
No trash in you."

Grandma!" I giggled. I couldn't have been more than eight.

Close to midnight, Grandmother and I were sitting on the porch. No, not really a porch. We were too poor for that. We were sitting on a stoop, a series of steps leading up to a front door with a vestibule to provide temporary shelter from the Pittsburgh winters. But the double set of doors locked in too much heat during sweltering summers. Our house lacked air-conditioning. Only fans, with steel mill soot settling as soon as you wiped them clean, stirred the humid air. It was too hot to sleep in the three-storied, crumbling brick house. So the family spent long summer nights sitting on the steps.

"Going to the porch," we'd say. "Sitting on the porch." "On the porch," we'd coo, feeling expansive, like we lived in an oasis rather than an industrial ghetto.

When it rained, our porch became a wet, slippery gray. But that didn't dampen our ownership pride. Anchored by the six concrete steps and foot-long landing, we, kids, lived recklessly and joyously.

On our porch we played jacks. In front of it, we played hopscotch, our squares drawn with colored chalk. We never fretted about skinned knees, bone-jarring hops.

When traffic slowed, we'd play Double Dutch in the street. Sometimes Grandmother would join us, and I'd laugh outrageously, thrilled to see her hair bobbing, her skirt and white apron ballooning like a girl's, before she'd go into the house to fry chicken or smother chipped beef with gravy.

We thought we were a typical family—though nothing like the Dick and Jane I'd read in my first-grade readers. They were white, we were brown; and nobody we knew said, "See, Spot, run."

Grandmother and her husband, Reverend, Rev for short,

ruled the roost. Rev was stepdad to my father and aunt, both single parents (my dad, divorced; my aunt, widowed because of a barroom brawl). Brother and sister had returned to their mother, children in tow. Two daughters for Pop—me and my sister, Tonie; a daughter and two sons (all under six) for Aunt Delores—Aleta, Jerome, and James. All of us folks strained the contours of the house. There was never a place to just be. Never any privacy. You were always running into, stumbling over someone. The bathroom was the only place that guaranteed solitude, but even then, a knock would arrive and a thin voice call, spiking high, "I've got to go. Please."

Dad worked day shift; my aunt worked nights as a nursing assistant. Rev, on weekdays, poured molten steel and, on weekends, preached gospel for any church in need of a temporary preacher.

Grandmother, stuffing us with food, surrounding us with love, was the glue holding us all together.

Our Pittsburgh sky was always overcast with gray steel flakes. Our roads were broken cobblestone with faded metal tracks for clackity-clack streetcars. Fourth of July, we placed cherry bombs in the tracks, hearing them burst while the driver cursed and clanged his bell.

Inside our house, there was always a warm glow. A sense of forgiveness, understanding that we were children and were expected to raise a ruckus.

Grandma could holler, "Pick up your shoes"; "Scrape your plate"; "Don't slide down that banister again"; "Watch your mouth!" and make us still feel loved.

At night, our neighborhood became mythical. A long, thin street with weak streetlamps, bright fireflies, and soulful aromas of collards and fatback, fried onions, and sugar snap peas. A magical place where for an all-too-brief time, Grandmother raised me and taught me about life.

I didn't realize we were poor. Didn't know that other neighborhoods didn't have rats as big as cats. Wasn't everyone behind in taxes, mortgage payments yet, no matter what, paid the two dollars for burial insurance and fifty cents to hit the numbers?

"I dreamt number eight—play that."

"Six. Nine. Two. Six-nine-two. Rolls off your tongue like butter."

"My daughter's birthday is eleven July. My birthday's

five August. One-one-five. That oughta win at least a dollar."

Whoever hit the numbers gave a chitlin' party. Grandmother won the most, so she always kept a supply of frozen chitlins, hot sauce, and crackers.

"Cleanliness is godliness," she'd say, defrosting the chitlins under cold water. I swore I'd never eat those nasty, smelly things. Pig innards. Old-time slave food. The leftovers that Master threw to his overworked slaves. But all the adults loved them, even though Grandmother had to wash them not once but twice, then three times clean.

Still, I knew what Grandmother meant.

Cleanliness meant you and your house were in order. Grandmother fought the never-ending struggle with soot, with mounds of laundry (including my father's bloodstained butcher uniforms), with flatware caked in dried grits, and greasy frying pans that needed scouring. The house was never clean. It was more than one woman could handle—struggling to care for an extended family. Grandmother couldn't work fast enough, hard enough to keep her house and nine bodies clean. But she fought the good fight.

"Let me see your ears."

I'd bow my pig-tailed head and fold my ears forward.

"Good."

I polished my patent leathers before church too. Took pride that my nails shined. My underwear was clean. And my shoes sparkled and clicked from metal taps on the heels.

When I was dumped into the bathtub with my sister, Tonie, and cousin Aleta, I never played splash, only scrubbed my knobby elbows, knees, and picked the lint from my belly button.

Was I Grandmother's favorite child? I like to think so. But it's a lie.

"Grandma don't play favorites. I love you all." Her children. Her children's children. Her neighbors. Her neighbors' children. Everyone was God's children. And Grandmother loved us all. Each and every one.

And because of her loving, the whole neighborhood loved her back. Called her "Grandma." Men would tip their hats, boys would sometimes bow, and girls and women would kiss her cheek like she was rare. And she was.

"Evening. Fine evening, Mrs. Thornton."

"Yes, praise Lord."

"It's been another good day."

"So saith the Lord: 'Be blessed and ye shall receive.' "

"Grandma Thornton, I love you."

"I love you too."

"Can I borrow sugar?"

"Anytime, baby. Anytime."

"I think I'm pregnant."

"Put your feet up. Call on the Lord."

Grandmother would listen to any troubles, but never gossiped. She was better than the confessional. She'd tell us children to "run and be hush" while she listened to secrets sinners were reluctant to tell God. Grandmother was in the flesh; nonetheless, when the session of confessing was done, Grandmother would remind the sinner, "Jesus loves you."

Summer nights, after a while, my youngest cousins would swoon, dry up like petals burned by too much sun. Rev would carry them to bed. A boy-child would be tucked under each arm. Afterward, he'd shuffle down the stairs and sit at the dining room table for hours, smoking Camels and drinking cold black coffee. This was a signal for Aleta and Tonie to scoot inside to watch late-night movies. Cagney, always a gangster, shouted, "Stick 'em up"; Bob Hope, goofy and drab, played a ukelele. They liked it best when Fred Astaire danced and spun his Ginger Rogers.

Grandmother and I would sit on the stoop, on the misnamed porch, studying the stars, the cars that turned onto our street, and neighbors, like us, trying to escape the heat. Sometimes, we'd snap pole beans for tomorrow's dinner, or wave fans with photos of a white Christ crucified. Or a rosy-cheeked Mary looking serenely at her baby.

If I pressed her, Grandmother would play hand clap games. "Miss Mary Mack, Mack, Mack. She asked her mother, mother, mother . . . for fifty cents, cents, cents . . . to see the elephant, elephant, elephant . . ." My small hands smacked against her calloused hands: "Jump over the fence, fence, fence . . ."

When I tired of Miss Mack, I insisted we do a few rounds of "A sailor went to sea, sea, sea to see what he could see, see, see . . ." I must've driven Grandmother mad. Yet she always said yes to my silly games. "Jewell, child, yes." Hearing Grandmother whisper those three words summed up all my comfort, my joy at being safe within the boundaries of her love. "Jewell. Child. Yes."

Even when Grandmother was young, I believed she was old. Truth be told, life had taken its toll on her body—diabetes, high blood pressure. Her upper register was filled with fake porcelain teeth. Years of sacrifice as a single parent (before she married Rev), then more years of making sure her children's children had—whether it be food, medical care, a roof over their heads—had taken its toll. Only ageless thing was her love. Her spirit was young like her soul.

I cherished my outside time with Grandmother, pinching myself both to stay awake and for sheer happiness at being alone with her.

I always sensed Grandmother was happy, too, enjoying her respite from the day, even though she'd be up again by six.

"Tell me stories."

"I've told you before."

"Tell me again." And she'd hug me to her bosom and never fail to oblige. "Did I tell you the blackbird's tale?"

"Yes. Tell me again. Tell me like you told me the first time."

She'd smack her gums. And I swear a hush fell shimmering, straight down from the sky.

"This is an old, old tale. My mother told me. Her mother told her."

We were cocooned on the porch: Grandmother, sitting tall on the top step; me, sitting one step below, my chin even with her knees.

"Blackbirds were the slaves who flew back to Africa. Every time you see a blackbird, you should think of a slave who set himself free."

"Have blackbirds always been ex-slaves?"

"No. Didn't begin until two centuries ago. Eighteen hundreds, down in Alabama. Hundreds of slaves were picking cotton, suffering under Master's care, all of them singing about the need to go. Singing about 'Crossing the River Jordan.' Or 'Go Down Moses, let my people go.' All these Christian songs they'd been taught. They sang, too, about trains and 'How long they'd been gone? Baby, how long?' But only so many could take the Underground Railroad. Only so many could escape. Most just sang, mournful, wailing, filled with never-ending yearning.

"The oldest slave was a spell man. He knew about herbs, how to mix possets and teas. One day, when the sorrowful songs seemed to rock the sky, the old man put down his hoe, shouting, 'Children, remember. Remember who you be.'

"The slaves were bewildered. They'd forgotten who they were. Couldn't remember any name before they were called Sally. Mary. Tom or Joe.

"The old man, his back bowed, crisscrossed with scars, looked at the dulled faces, the thin men and women, hands calloused from cotton, the children, heavy-lidded and tired, and said, 'Time to go. Time to go.' He whispered his African name in the nearest slave's ear. Whispered his name deep down into the other slave's soul. Then, he raised his arms toward the sun and flew. Just lifted off the ground. His arms became wings. His back grew feather-down. His legs elongated into feet with talons. 'High,' he said. 'High beyond the horizon. I'm free.'

"Other slaves began whispering their African names. Olun, Nambi, Membe, raising their arms and believing in their power to fly. Straight at the sun. Through puffs of clouds. No worries about wings burning off. Just soaring, straight and high. Far into the sky.

"The overseer was bewildered, riding his horse, cracking his whip like a madman. Threatening any slave who tried to rise. He knew Master would fire him for even one slave lost. He grabbed John's foot, only to have talons draw blood. 'Kailila,' John cried, long and hard, the vowels turning into a high-pitched screech. The overseer shook his fist at John/Kailila. Shook his fist at the swarm of blackbirds diving through clouds, creating swirls of black on bright blue sky.

"When there was a flock, over two dozen slaves turned into sleek blackbirds, they turned as one and headed east—back across the ocean, the wide, wide expanse of restless waters, to the African shore."

"All the slaves flew?"

"No, some slaves were left behind. They wished the black-birds well. Clapped their hands. Shouted out a farewell song."

"Didn't they cry?"

"Sure they did. Sometimes too much pain can make you forget pieces of yourself. Forget your homeland, the people you loved. Slavery's outrageous curse. But the remaining slaves were left to tell the tale. Like my grandparents. They saw the blackbirds fly. They told the tale, passing it on and on and down to me. Me, passing it to you."

"Did the blackbirds become human again?"

"You mean when their feet touched the soil?"

"Yes," I sighed, wishing my arms would become wings and I could fly into the night sky, soaring above tenement houses, Pittsburgh's three rivers and rolling hills.

"Yes, but some of the slaves, having crossed the sea, preferred to fly. They no longer wanted to be on land where they could be captured and resold. They preferred life as winged creatures, feeling the sun bake their black wings.

"Sunshine never scorches them. They never fall. Never drown in the sea. Just call—sometimes with pain, sometimes with alarm—sometimes with plain melancholy. Some say they call for their lost families, for mothers and fathers they couldn't return to, for brothers and sisters enslaved. Sometimes they call—caw—hurting, because they feel the depth of human pain. They remember their buried pain, piercing way down deep, just as they remember their original names. Some say they call for all the slaves that died at sea. Those that never survived the crossing.

"Most times, slaves were tossed overboard if they were too weak, too sick to fetch a good price. Sometimes, whole cargos—men, women, and children—were drowned when a

British ship chased the slavers. No cargo, no crime. Their caw-cawing keep the drowned souls from feeling lonely.

"What blackbirds like best is sitting in a treetop, atop a wire, or on a scarecrow's hat, watching the neat rows of growing corn. Sun, Earth, and Water keep on providing. Blackbirds keep true to their freedom. Before sleeping, before tucking their heads beneath their wings, they give a special call—caw-caw. Caw-caw. Call-call."

"Call, what? What do they say? What's the cawing mean?"

"That's the secret. Call. Caw-caw. Some say the birds keep repeating their African names. They say they do it before sleep, to make certain they won't forget. In case they ever decide to be human again.

"Some say the blackbirds caw/call, carrying tales. They call for you and me to travel homeward, to hold on to our selves despite hardship, despite pain. They caw-caw for us to pass down tales, down through the generation. They caw-caw for us to call upon our human selves to remember old truths . . . to remember a time when our ancestors left bitterness and pain, and rose up and flew as glorious blackbirds."

Each night Grandmother would tell a different tale . . . then, on Sunday, begin all over again. Sometimes she'd tell the same tales, sometimes she'd tell old tales redone. Sometimes there'd be an unexpected story. New and fresh beyond measure.

Porch stories didn't happen September through May. School nights were bland, filled with getting ready for tomorrows that echoed the same old day. Only during oppressive summer nights, when heat and humidity made the air too thick to breathe, did the soul-stirring stories arise. Each year, they'd change a bit, as if the stories changed according to my age. Different details would be filled in from six to eight or eight to ten. In truth, Grandmother's stories were for all ages. But the tales themselves were like labyrinths, mazes, where the meaning wasn't always clear.

Everything came with a maxim:

"Jewell, child, what goes around, comes around."
"Reap what you sow."
*"Do unto others as you would have them
do unto you."*
"Do good and it'll fly right back to you."
"Catch your spirit up in a world of joy."

"The dead are with us. You're never alone. All things alive."

"Nobody in the world better than you. You no better than anyone else. We all a 'mixed-blood stew.'"

"Cry, then get on with it."

"Signs everywhere. Pay attention."

"Scratch a wall, somebody dies."

"Burn your hair, for if a bird finds it, uses it for its nest, your hair will fall right out."

"Small actions mean *something."*

"Every good-bye ain't gone."

"What's worth holding on to in this world sometimes can't be caught. Can't be held."

"Babies mean life."

I didn't understand half of what Grandmother said. Just marveled at her throaty laugh, her smacking gums. Her kind eyes. Tough hands.

I felt like the black sky was going to swallow me up—warm, comforting in its infinity and blackness. The complicated labyrinth of stories would never end. A communion existed between us; I knew how to be quiet, in love with

Grandmother's words and stories. Our small stoop became a universe.

She taught me how to live.

Remember your name. Who-you-be.
Be in love with your good self.

Wear clean underwear. Don't let anyone
ever think there's trash in you.

"Never underestimate feelings."

Y ou mean like angry?"

"No, I mean like love."

It was just the two of us. The air was breathing sweat. The moon was fat. Inside, the television glowed like another small moon. Outside, there was only Grandmother and me. It was time for a tale. Grandmother was looking far past the black horizon, and I was staring at the fireflies dancing like crazed lanterns in between the dim lampposts and parked cars.

"Down South, we had real porches. Porches that wrapped around the house like a mother's arms. Porches with pillars and posts. Rocking chairs and swings."

"Nice." I imagined my legs, kicking off a good swing, my body tilting forward and back.

"Down South, in Carolina," Grandmother clicked, smacking her toothless gums. (Her choppers were in the bathroom, in a tall glass with fizzy water bubbling them clean.)

"Down South," she said, ever wistful, "everybody was good to everybody else. Know why?"

She didn't wait for me to answer.

" 'Cause nobody had nothing. Not a thing. 'Not a pot to piss me in,' as my Daddy would say. 'Course we all had pots. We'd stuff them with the dandelion greens we found in the fields. Sometimes, we were lucky and had squirrel." She paused, squinting her eyes at something I couldn't see.

"Now what was I saying?"

"Pots," I giggled.

Grandmother smiled. "Yes, we all had pots. Used them when it was too cold to go to the outhouse. But even when it was steaming outside, in the middle of the night, my brothers sometimes didn't bother with the outhouse."

I blushed. Hearing Grandmother talk about the bathroom tickled me.

"Never mind that we all shared one big room."

I smothered a shriek, and Grandmother pulled my pigtail.

"You didn't really cook in the same pots, did you? You know, that your brothers used?"

"Country ways different than city ways."

My eyes widened.

" 'Course not. 'It's a saying,' as my beloved Daddy would say. 'Not a pot to—" She held her finger to her mouth, silencing the word. I bit my tongue.

"Country ways different than city ways," said Grandmother. " 'Course this was 1926. Down South . . ."

"Down South," I echoed.

"Everyone was good to everyone else."

"Good," I repeated solemnly, then sucked on an ice cube sprinkled with salt. We lived up North. In a city that glowed from industrial mills (spewing smoke and orange light from mammoth furnaces), from sky-high wires sparking with electricity. We lived in a city with more concrete than live, growing things.

Grandmother rubbed her knees. They ached, I knew, from trumping up and down stairs, day and night, dawn to dusk. They ached even more that day, as Grandmother had gone fetching, bustling in the kitchen, cooking good food for all of us, but especially for Rev. He'd come home with strike news. All the black and brown men were on alert. They knew that when there was trouble, they'd be sacrificed. "First fired, last hired or rehired." Reverend, by taking the most dangerous jobs, hoped to keep us safe. Secure. Not many wanted to do what he did—handling molten steel, rivers of blood-black lava fire. He prayed all the time. Before and after work; lunch time, snack time; in between tense minutes of work. Grateful each day he hadn't been scarred, maimed, or killed.

Tonight, after dinner, he sat at the table, chain-smoking, his bushy brows shading, hiding his gaze. Us kids were told to be quiet and to step gently around him. My boy cousins took themselves off to bed. Unheard of. As if they'd known before it could happen, that they'd be too raucous and loud. Rev would roar, towering, shouting, passionate preacher-style, about spoiled children and "spare rods." Tonie and Aleta sat cross-legged on the floor, close to the TV, its sound whispery low so Rev wouldn't hear. Every hour or so, Rev would jolt out of his reverie, saying, "Electric bill." "Car note." "Groceries."

Men folk had it hard. Women folk, harder? I don't know if Grandmother would've said that. But Rev got to sit and worry while Grandmother catered, rubbed his shoulders, and tempted him with fresh tomatoes and strawberry pie. She just kept going—scraping dishes, drying silverware, shaking out the tablecloth, sweeping the dining room and kitchen floors, never stopping, never resting 'til late, later, ever so late, when she plumped down on the stoop, outside, on the porch, with me.

She'd already told Rev a dozen times not to worry about bills: "You're a good provider." She didn't say once "Black men get paid less." Nor did she let him see worry furrowing around her lips, brows, and eyes. Rev only saw her smile—generous, encouraging, and kind. She patted and kissed his brow, inhaling his special aroma—Old Spice, tobacco, and soot.

Grandmother stretched her toes, wiggling them like they were in water. She still had her apron on. Her hair glowed silver. Then she let her eyelids droop, her head tilt slightly, and she seemed to stare well beyond the city's blackness. I knew Grandmother was seeing grass, flowers, and trees of her South. Maybe even smelling magnolias, swamp pools, and compost ripening, nurturing plants.

"Down South," she murmured, and the sound rose like the fireflies, then dropped off in a sigh.

"Down South, down South," I chanted. It was the magical

place where Grandmother grew up . . . way down in Carolina land.

" 'Didn't have a pot to piss in.' "

"Your Daddy would say."

"That's right. Didn't have nothin'."

"That's right."

"All you needed was what's in your mind. Heart. Soul. I've done told you before?" Her voice pitched high.

"You've done told me before."

Her arms, thin, yet as strong as reeds, reached around me. My back to her bosom, she held me tight. Cheek pressed to cheek.

"All you need is what's in your mind. Your heart . . ."

" 'Your heart,' " I mouthed in unison.

"Your soul."

" 'Your soul.' " The words singed the air.

My head dropped and I squirmed, burrowing more deeply into Grandmother's chest. Her heart soothed with its steadiness.

"Having is never a substitute for feeling. You feel, you be alive. Having just means another thing you aren't taking to heaven. Did I ever tell you about Mrs. Abby?"

"Naw."

"I didn't tell you about how Mrs. Abby became a widow?"

Of course she had. Sometimes I answered, "Yes. I've heard it before. Tell me again." Sometimes I said no. Like it was the first time. This was part of our game. Part of our ritual.

Tonight I answered, "No, tell me."

"Well, I'll tell you." She scrunched her lips, took a deep inhale.

"Mr. Abby grew the finest peaches. Acres of peach trees, plump and juicy, and he sold them by the roadside. Sold them all his life. He was an old man. But each evening, during the sultry summers, he liked to bring the sweetest, just plucked from the tree, to Mrs. Abby.

"He'd shutter his roadside stand. Count his coins. Then he'd go back into the fields and search for the best peach. He'd move his ladder from tree to tree, 'cause as he often said, 'Cain't tell the best 'til you're way up close.' Sometimes, he'd be picking for fifteen minutes, a half an hour, or more. Mrs. Abby used to tell him she'd rather have more time with him at home than the very best peach. But Mr. Abby was stubborn. Said peach season was short. Said to anyone who would listen, 'Mrs. Abby slicing a peach is a beautiful thing to see.'

"They say his fingers clasped the yellowest, biggest, and best peach. The peach shook itself; it didn't want to be picked, preferred to rot and fall to the ground. Some say: 'Sun got in his eyes. Lost his balance. Fell. Broke his neck. Just died in his grove.' Others say: 'Just his time. Who knows what gave out? His heart, mind? Him and his wife, old wrinkled folks—like peaches left too long in the sun.'

"The Abbys were dirt poor. Land rich. Without a pot. They'd always been poor. Just as there'd always been a community to help. Women baking an extra loaf of bread, men cutting an extra cord of wood. Everybody in town and on farms were poor, but the Abbys were the poorest of the poor. Everybody cared for them like family.

"When Mr. Abby died, things were no different. Folks brought pies—no peach. Brought chicken, potato salad enough for a houseful of children. All of Mrs. Abby's children were dead—one from pneumonia, another drowned in a creek bed.

"All the men folks talked about having to provide more. 'Be a stand-in for her husband.' Not just food and wood. A little coal. Kerosene oil. Help with the orchards.

"Women talked about providing company. 'Hard for a

woman to be alone and poor.' Both were too much. 'Not a
child or grandchild to rescue her.'

"I'll be there for you, Grandmother."

"I know it. You've got country ways. But townsfolk wor-
ried, too, about inheritors. They hoped for distant relations.
Word had it that the county wanted the land, wanted to sell to
developers to build houses black folks couldn't afford to own.

"Jewell, child, living is always hard. Not just for blacks . . .
everybody's got their own row to hoe. Back then, we thought
it was Mrs. Abby. All of us feeling sorry for her—poor, black,
and a woman alone. But she showed us what riches were. She
had a lifetime of thoughts and feelings that made her far richer
than any of us knew."

Grandmother rubbed her left side, beneath her heart.

"Sunset, Mr. Abby was buried on his land. Right between
rows of his beloved peach-blooming trees. After the funeral,
we all followed Mrs. Abby back to the porch for dinner. Passing plates piled high with deviled eggs, sliced tomatoes, corn
relish, powder biscuits, chicken, and smoked ham. Lemonade
washed it all down.

"Everybody told tales about Mr. Abby.

"Abraham said, 'He was always a Mister from the day he

was born. Nobody dared call him Charlie. *Charles* was tolerated, but soon as he was tall, thin, and sixteen, everyone started calling him Mister. He was always so dignified.' Abraham wiped his eyes. He'd known Mr. Abby since their sporadic attendance in third grade. Both needed to drop out to farm. 'His name was Charles, did you know that?' Abraham stabbed his walking stick into the ground, propping himself up.

"Preacher Howard told how Mr. Abby wasn't a churchgoing man. 'But every summer, he'd bring a harvest of peaches for my wife to set by. Though he wasn't churchgoing, he was church feeling.'

" 'Amen,' said many a neighbor.

"Then someone else stood, his voice quivering. 'I once had my leg broke and Mr. Abby, he was younger then, spent weeks turning my soil, planting my new crop. We would've starved.'

" 'He was a good, good man,' everyone said.

" 'Amen,' rose again.

" 'Mr. Abby bought licorice for my kids,' said a freckled-face man. 'He'd gone to town, had a few pennies to spare, and bought red and black vines. Dropped them all in a bag for my kids to share. No reason. Just kindness. They never had so many sweets. Not even Christmas.'

"When all the folks were full of food and stories, they sat down, leaned against posts, laid on blankets atop the grass. Light from the house streamed out. Moths batted at the porch lights. The stars twinkled bravely. And kids clasped glowing jars of lightning bugs. That's when Mrs. Abby closed her eyes and said, 'I remember . . .'

"Everybody hushed. Mrs. Abby told tales all night long. I was a child myself, but I remember. Her, in the rocking chair, the air wafting with blooming fruit. Mr. Abby's fresh grave just a few feet away, tucked beneath the trees.

"Mrs. Abby had never talked much, but that night she did. Testifying. All the men and boys seemed to know they should disappear. They went to smoke cheroots, drink moonshine, hard liquor. The boys played hide-and-seek.

"All the women appeared, ready to listen. Some sat on kitchen chairs pulled outside onto the porch, some sat on the porch steps, some on the swing. Some lay on the blankets stretched across the grass. Girls gathered round too. Babies suckled, and toddlers pulled up clumps of grass. Bigger girls, like me, kept still, knowing we were lucky to hear our mothers, aunts, and grandmothers talk. Everyone was solemn, like in church.

" 'I remember Charles.' Mrs. Abby's voice trembled as old voices sometimes do. 'Tall, strapping boy. Eyes pale as a blue marble. Looked like a cataract man. Though he weren't but seventeen. I was crazy about him. Nice thighs. Long, lanky arms. Good rear.'

"Women laughed and I giggled, but I never guessed they were talking about longing sparking between a woman and a man.

" 'When he turned eighteen, he asked Pa to marry me. Asked Pa before he asked me.' You could still hear Mrs. Abby's pleased outrage. 'I was told to sit on the sofa. Be still and be quiet while Pa asked about Charles's prospects.'

" 'None,' he said, 'except what my hands and back can give.'

" 'Pa refused him,' saying, 'You ain't got a pot to piss in.'

" 'But just 'cause I was sitting on the sofa didn't mean Pa was going to decide everything. I wore him down. First, I stopped feeding the chicks and pigs. Then, I stopped making his favorite cobbler. I put pepper in his tobacco. Then I laid in bed for a week, curtains drawn, and moaned whenever he poked his head in. Mama told him I wasn't eating, but she hid a tray of apples and cheese beneath my bed.'

" 'Finally, Pa said, "Fine. Marry him. It's better than watching you die." '

" 'I hopped out of bed, kissed Pa, then rode our nag to Charles's house. I insisted he ask me what I was going to do about marrying him. Charles hemmed and hawed. Said he respected my Daddy. I said, "Respect me." '

" 'He gave a slow smile.'

" 'You should have asked me in the first place.'

" 'Will you?'

" 'I will.'

" 'Then, I kissed him hard.'

"I could see Mrs. Abby all pretty and petite, fussing at her beau, then kissing him. Though she was frail, past eighty-three, she still held her beauty in her sweet face.

" 'At the wedding, Charles gave me a perfect string. "Here. For you." It was a half-foot long. Blistering white. He tied it round my finger, whispering, "I do." '

" 'Pa was disgusted. Most thought it was funny, but, to me, the string was precious like gold.'

"In my mind's eye, I could see the newlyweds. The

string—a promise of simple perfection, of threads bound beautifully like their lives.

" 'Married days not always easy,' Mrs. Abby went on. 'Days were hard, trying to scratch a living from the orchards. Had nothing. Just our dreams and saplings needing tending.'

" 'In the evenings, the string was our only entertainment. We played like children. Cat's Cradle. Witch's broom. Cup and Saucer. Then, we played together in bed like God expected grown lovers to do.' "

Grandmother smiled, tugging my pigtail. I smiled too.

" 'We used the string to tie off the umbilical cords of our two babies. But neither lived past eight. One drowned in a creek bed, a mystery. I still don't know how he got there. One caught pneumonia.'

"Mrs. Abby bowed her head. Times were hard down South. Sometimes we only had flour and water. But my mama, your great-grandmother, had all her babies live. Mrs. Abby went on:

" 'Every night, we'd read the Bible. Luke our favorite. Every night, Mr. Abby held me; I held him. Even when our spirits were low, when our arms ached from toiling, when our bodies were wrinkled and not so pretty.'

" 'No,' the women said. 'You're beautiful.'

"Mrs. Abby waved her hand, waving away their words like shooflies. 'We kept the string in an old honey pot on the mantel, right beneath a cross.'

"Mrs. Abby reached in her dress pocket and pulled out a wriggling string like a snake from a charmer's basket. It twisted, glowed against the black air, like it had a life of its own. Frayed at the edges, smaller than when it was brand new. Frayed from use and washing.

"The women cooed and sighed.

" 'Little things,' said Mrs. Abby, her voice filled with breath and sorrow. 'A peach. A twig from a bird's nest. A pebble he found in the fields. Charles was always bringing me little things. Things he spent time selecting, knowing how much his little things would bring me pleasure. But the string was my favorite. It was an everlasting way of him telling me that he loved me.'

" 'Just a piece of string to seal nearly seventy years of loving.'

"Everyone was envious of the everlasting gift.

" 'When we had nothing,' Mrs. Abby said, 'he'd pull it out and gift it to me all over again. Or, for the children, on Christmas, when nothing was to be had . . . oh, I remember . . . how we played with the string. Glory, peace, fun, and care. All rolled up together in twine. What we didn't have, didn't matter. When Daniel took sick, we kept the string by his bed. Played with it as Danny became more and more weak.'

" 'When Billy went missing, the string was all we had . . . and it was really a blessing. Kept us feeling, steeped like mint leaves in warm water, in touch with memories, our feelings for each other. Didn't need to have anything else. It helped us grieve.'

"Mrs. Abby paused, burying her face in her hands. Then, she stood and all of us stood, too, gathering round. Babies stopped crying, mosquitoes hovered, not daring to draw blood. Even the stars stopped twinkling.

"Mrs. Abby dangled the string from her fingers. She stood regal, a petite but proud bird of a woman. I think she forgot any of us were there.

" 'All he had to give, and it was enough. All I have and it should be enough.'

"Then she looked at me, 'specially, I thought. Then she looked at each of the mothers-daughters-sisters-cousins-aunts in turn.

" 'I'm going to lay down and think of him.'

"Next morning, my mama and I went to check on her. Mrs. Abby had flown to glory. The honey pot nestled on the bed beside her pillow. The last peach her husband brought her was still on the nightstand with a paring knife. Some say she laid down and just went to sleep. Others, that she missed her marriage games. She died smiling. Like she fully expected to be with Charles and her boys, Billy and Daniel.

"My mama opened the honey pot. Inside, the piece of string was cut into tiny pieces. A note nestled on its side."

Thank you all.

"Mrs. Abby had written in shaky script."

"How to know if a man loves you? String. How to show your love? String. But that ain't all of it, Jewell, girl. Mrs. Abby was telling all of us that feelings, memories . . . being together, having love in this world is more important than anything.

"Rich in feeling, Widow Abby laid down to sleep."

Grandmother sighed. "Time to get Rev some rest. Time to massage his brow."

"Have you and Rev got strings?"

Grandmother smiled. "No. But we got dancing."

"I've never seen you."

"You don't need to see. But we dance. Have danced. We can look into each other's eyes and do a whole jitterbug. That's our string, our memories."

"Let me see."

"It's not something I need to show."

"I know. But I want to see. Pleassse." I drawled out the *s* and blinked my eyes like a puppy. Grandmother pinched my cheek.

"Maybe I should." She smacked her thighs and all her weariness fell away; her joints seemed loose and limber.

I followed her into the house. Rev always looked like a black Moses to me. Though he was good to Grandmother's children and grandchildren, I never bothered him more than I had to. He was always somber, grouchy, and righteous all at the same time.

"Let's dance."

"Woman, you crazy."

"Naw." Grandmother was holding out her arms. Her face glowing like a girl's. "Dance with me."

He was stern, looking at Grandmother like she'd lost her mind; then he smiled. A slow grin that matched Grandmother's.

Tonie and Aleta had left the TV on. They were jumping up and down on the sofa. Nobody yelled. Truth be, Rev and Grandmother didn't seem to see anybody else except each other.

I was standing in the doorway to the dining room. I watched, my heart quickening, toes tingling, as they danced round the dining room table, around the chairs, over the toy trucks scattered on the floor—as they danced through the pantry, straight into the kitchen, round the hallway to the vestibule, and came bobbing side to side, behind me.

They started another round, with stares only for each other, listening to silent yet thrilling music. They two-stepped back through the pantry, into the kitchen, and, following them, I saw Grandmother take Rev's hand and pull him outside to the back porch, a thin, L-shaped concrete yard with a bit of dirt and two Blanche Mallerin rosebushes growing in pots.

I didn't go outside. I figured Grandmother and Rev were making up their own tale.

Never underestimate feelings. Love is expressed by "little things." Peaches. String. A two-step or slow jitterbug. Even friends helping you through rough times with seemingly small kindnesses needed celebrating.

I went back outside, sat on the front stoop. I could hear Grandmother's voice whispering inside my head, *Come on, Rev. Let's dance.*

Much, much later, Grandmother took me off to bed. She'd put everybody to bed. Even Rev. He probably slept with a smile, no longer worrying about union troubles and bills.

Grandmother came to claim me. She tucked the covers between the mattress and the springboard and stroked my hair.

"If you feel, your spirit is rich. A mind should be filled with memories. A heart should be filled with love. That's how we tried to live down South. That's how I seen folks die."

Grandmother kissed me on the cheek, murmuring like a honeybee caressing my ear, "Down South. Down South. Not a pot to piss in. Still, the community gave what it could.

"Mr. Abby gave all that was needed. 'Little things' add up to big. You remember that, Jewell, girl."

I did. Remembered every word.

Never underestimate the power of feelings.
Being well-loved means good memories.

A piece of string can be more precious than
a rope of pearls.

"Jewell, child, you never need

an excuse for joy."

I understood this maxim well. It mattered to remember that life was wonderful—that in between the string of bad times, there were good days, good moments to cherish.

Old Mr. Allen used to say, "If you're breathing, life's good."

Rev would reply, "If you've been good and you're dead, the afterlife is even better."

I always tried to be good. I took to heart that life was joyful. Meant to be cherished. Sometimes it was hard. I knew my mother left when I was a not-even-crawling infant. Most days, I imagined she'd miss me enough to come back. Most nights, I speculated about the various traumas that kept her away. She was ill with fever, lost in farthest Africa without a ticket home, kidnapped by pirates who admired her beauty and talent.

Mornings would begin a fresh round of hopefulness. Silliness even, for I'd been told over and over again, mother didn't love my father anymore. It was unlikely that she'd ever come back.

Like an unforgiving ache, knowing my mother hadn't loved me enough to stay . . . hadn't loved me enough to take me with her, I would have sad days. Sometimes I'd hide in the closet, buried beneath piles of winter coats. I'd listen as everybody called for me: "Jewell." "Jewell, child." "Grandma's going to whip you." "I'll tell Dad." "Where are you?" "Jewell, come out this instant!!!"

Eventually, I'd come out. Grandmother would hug me like crazy. I'd pretend I was lost, and now I was found. My cousins would roll their eyes and stick out their tongues. I basked in Grandmother's love. It made me feel worthy to know I'd been missed, and no matter how many times I hid, no matter how many times they didn't find my hiding place, it never failed to reassure me that Grandmother missed me and wanted me found.

Still, I liked to lie in bed, on the third floor, waking slowly to the sunlight cutting across my room. There were three twin beds in a row for me, my sister, and Aleta. I often felt we were the three bears. I was middle bear, listening to our house groaning awake.

Grandmother puttered in the kitchen, making coffee and lunch for Rev. Pop was long gone. Aunt Delores was still sleeping off the graveyard shift. There'd be soft murmurs; then, Rev would clank his thermos and metal lunch box and walk out the double vestibule doors and down our porch steps to his beloved Chevy.

The rocking horse in front of my bedroom window would seem less battered, less rusty as the sun crept higher. Through the lace curtains, I could see treetops, rooftops, and, I thought, way off in the distance, the steel mill chimneys spewing smoke. I liked to imagine I could see beyond anything. I had X-ray vision like Superman, eyes piercing beyond the horizon, following the slope of Pittsburgh's hills, past Allegheny Park, an oasis for playing, and down toward the banks where three rivers—Susquehanna, Monongahela, and Allegheny—met.

I'd wiggle my toes, stretch and arch my back, then pause and wait expectantly. Hearing the echo of Grandmother going up and down the basement steps, carrying loads of laundry, boiling Argo starch on the stove, I could tell how her body felt. If I barely heard her, just the basement door squeaking open and closed, I knew she didn't ache much. If I heard heavy footsteps and sometimes shuffling, then I knew arthritis was hurting her knees and her lower back ached.

Sometimes I'd wait ten minutes snug in bed, sometimes twenty, sometimes minutes longer, even half an hour. Tonie would be a lump, dead to the world. Aleta would be twisted in the sheets, slightly snoring, her leg dangling off the bed.

I'd pull my sheet up to my chin and wait for the sound, the

call, the holler, the tune that didn't come as often as I'd like. Never knew what set it off. Maybe the sunrays on the linoleum, a butterfly alighting on Grandmother's roses, maybe no pain in Grandmother's joints, maybe too much pain. When the call came, it filled my soul with joy.

It would start with a hum floating up from the cavern of the stairwell. Snatches of dissonant sound. Then there'd be a phrase: "Your Momma may have, your Papa may have . . ." The chorus was sung over and over; then, finally, Grandmother's voice soaring from low to high, alto to soprano, soft to loud . . . a singing that tore and stirred my soul like in church sometimes.

When Rev wasn't around, Grandmother sang secular tunes: blues, work chants, "Summertime" from *Porgy and Bess*.

I often wondered if Grandmother forgot about us grandkids sleeping far and high away upstairs. But she never did.

> *Your Momma may have,*
> *Your Papa may have.*
> *But God bless the child*
> *Who's got her own.*

When I could stand it no longer, when her song had un-settled and refreshed me, I'd tiptoe out of bed, sit at the top of the stairs, peering through the banister, the cavern of three flights. Soon, Grandmother would stop, look up, her hand on the rail, and say, "Block Party Day." Mind you, not every day, maybe twice during a summer. Most times, she'd say, "Up and at 'em. Grits. You want 'em wet, dried, or fried?"

I tried to figure out the logic of Block Party days. Was it the quality of air? A combination of temperature, humidity? Direction of the wind? Hot days, high moisture, a light breeze from the west? Or was it the number of birds outside, chirping in trees? Or something else? A lassitude? A message sparked by the flutter of a curtain? A hint of a faraway storm? Or an un-canny calm? Was I too young to recognize the subtle hints, the signs when Grandmother knew, like no one else knew, it was the time for a Block Party Day?

I'd tumble down the stairs to be embraced by Grand-mother.

"Hurry. Let me eat."

"Clean your face and hands first."

My job was town crier.

In truth, anyone could call Block Party Day, but when Grandmother did it, it was extra special, as if everyone knew her sincerity, her wisdom, knew she was imbued with ancient magic.

Sunset streaked the sky bright pink and orange, thanks to J. L. Steel. Always on Grandmother's Block Party days, the sunset was filled with rainbows.

I ate cold cereal instead of grits and walked across the street to Mrs. Chalmers's house. She was already on her porch, sitting on a plastic chair, studying her neighbors. It was her major entertainment. When I whispered, "Block Party Day," she clapped her hands, declaring, "I'll make my fried chicken." Grandmother's chicken was better. Nonetheless, Mrs. Chalmers enjoyed spending the morning watching oil gurgle and chicken brown. When it cooled, she'd sprinkle it with Lawry's Seasoned Salt and fresh ground pepper.

Grandmother baked cornbread—trays and trays of ground meal mixed with butter, sugar, and eggs.

I went from house to house, knocking on doors, seeing women in pink curlers, old men in long johns, kids dulled by TV cartoons, and dogs wagging their tails because someone had arrived on their doorstep. They'd all beam like it was Christmas when I chirped, "Block Party Day."

Mr. Berry, who had a splotch of pink roses on his cheeks and liked checkers, nearly kicked his heels together when I announced, "Block Party."

"I'll make a run for ice." He grinned, in seventh heaven, knowing he'd spend much of his day carrying his lawn chair, roaming the street for a checkers partner. He'd play with most everyone, even my cousin, Aleta, who, at five, had to be told nearly every move.

Then I spied Jim, home on leave from the army, his head stuck into an engine. He had on his clodhopper shoes. Everybody loved good-natured Jim. "Jim, my car stalled." "Jim, can you drive me to the grocery?" "Jim, my sink is clogged." And Jim, with a matter-of-fact sweetness, would fix an engine, drive to the store, or pour Drano down an oil-slick pipe.

When he smiled, he was so handsome. My sister, Tonie, swore she'd marry him, but I was convinced he'd wait for me.

He'd pluck quarters from behind my ear and tell me I was going to grow up and "be a dream."

Jim was my dream. He played basketball, spinning, ducking and diving, and throwing hoops. I was his biggest fan.

"I'll go round the fire department," Jim said. "Get the guys to spread the word. Bring extra tables and chairs."

Then we grinned together, feeling like conspirators. For the fireman's real job was to let the hydrant blow.

I skipped off, at peace with the world. I'd done a day's work before my sister and cousins were awake.

Grandmother would let me wake them, screaming like a banshee, "BLOCK PARTY DAY."

The best Block Party days happened during weekdays. Mainly women, children, and old men played games, cooked, and chatted.

By midafternoon, we'd all be ready, eager for our loved ones to come home from work, surprised by Block Party Day. They'd be squirted with hoses and, if we were lucky, if the hydrant was spraying, us kids would squeal, giggle, stumble, and run through the powerful whoosh of water. Fat Petey dared us to inch closer to the hydrant, deep far in, to where the water became painful and knocked us down. Water met with oil slicks and made rainbows like the rainbows from our bottles of bubble. Small bubbles, large bubbles, and the littlest kids jumping, scurrying, catching, and popping them. Some held bubbles in their palms like precious gems. Others popped them; others blew bubbles across the sky.

Crows would perch on the trolley wires and watch us, their heads tilting left, then right, turning their beady eyes so that they could see better. I'd suspect they'd fly off with tales to tell, caw-cawing about our joy.

Grown-ups arrived, stripping away their work clothes. Grown men would take off their socks and shoes, and kick puddles of water. Women would fling off their heels, set aside their purses, and dash into the whirling ropes of a Double Dutch game.

Men kissed their wives, hugged their children. Pop would spin us round and round 'til we squealed, dizzier than wayward chickens. His face would be utterly relaxed, no creases of worry. Even Rev would park his car and smile. By evening time, he'd have his amiable preacher look, looking at God's children with indulgence and grace.

Then we'd all eat, going from porch to porch. Some set up card tables covered with paper napkins and corn ears bathed in margarine; others set tables on the sidewalk, bowlegged with heavy bowls of rice and beans; still others arranged chicken platters on concrete steps. It was a door-to-door, porch-to-porch banquet of summertime foods: watermelon slices, carrots sliced with pineapple and raisins, and, best of all, ice cream floating in Hawaiian Punch.

A hoop for pickup basketball was staked in an abandoned lot between the Moores' and the Pickneys' houses. It was dangerous to leap on uneven ground with rocks and slivers of glass, but no one minded. The game was fun and ferocious. My favorite was dodgeball. Seemed like the whole neighborhood picked teams and filled the street, tossing, throwing, rolling a ball to strike folks like pins. Afterwards, children would use squirt guns to cool off.

Husbands and wives seemed more generous in their affection. Knotty old men were sweeter, boasting about the "good ole days."

And Laila, who didn't pass a day without shouting at

and smacking her kids, kissed them gooey and talked about how they were "so cute," as if she'd been given rose glasses and saw some kids we didn't see. (We knew her kids were trouble . . . and though all us children got spanked, all of us, child and adult alike, believed her kids deserved it. Every good lick. 'Specially Tyrone and sassy Lenore.)

Night—when the streetlights magically blinked on—was the best. Grandmother hadn't done a stitch of laundry. My dad lifted the boy cousins high in the air, twirling me, Tonie, and Aleta like we were on the tornado at Kennywood Park. All of us kids were his.

The world was beautiful. We'd set the stage, drawing steps and lines with our colored chalk. Brooms became microphones. Tonie would run and get the tape player, and me, Tonie, and Aleta would become the Supremes. " 'Stop, in the name of love . . . before you break my heart . . .' " We'd shimmy our tails and wag our fingers and all the adults would clap, the other children scream. " 'Think it o-o-ver . . .' "

Before the moon was overhead, the Temptations, Martha

and the Vandellas, even the Dells had visited our neighbor-hood. Pop, small and wiry, acting drunk from too much glee, would become Smokey Robinson. Oh, how I loved him!

" 'People say I'm the life of the party . . .' " Pop crossed his hand over his heart. " '. . . tears of a clown.' " I wondered if he dreamt about my mother. Mainly I sighed, for Jim was one of the Miracles, and watching him and Pop sliding side to side, crossing their hearts and wiping their eyes, made my heart burst with love.

Cleanup was a mess, but everyone helped, even those who had to work the next day. That was the beauty of Block Party Day—it wasn't necessarily a convenient weekend. It just came and everyone stopped and enjoyed it to its fullest. Then, every-one took responsibility for making the carnival disappear. Every adult would be tired working the next day, but not a one would regret a second, a minute, an hour of Block Party Day. (Only us kids got to lie abed late, dreaming of sweets, songs, laughter, and games.)

Way late, maybe two o'clock, me and Grandmother reigned on the porch stoop. Jerome was curled in her lap, his head threatening to drop off his shoulder as sleep made his limbs like Jell-O.

Tonie was playing jacks, a flashlight on the concrete lighting her small arena. Aleta was asleep, sprawled on a blanket, on the last step. Both had foresworn their midnight movies.

"Today was fine," Grandmother said. A hum was curling out of the depths of her throat.

"Happy?" I asked.

"Yes. Very." She stilled Jerome's bobbing head against her shoulder. "More than that. Joyful."

"Joyful."

"Bigger than happiness."

"Big." And I thought of the bigness, the power of Pittsburgh's three rivers merging into the Ohio. How we all had come together and done a good thing. Made life special.

"Joy," I repeated, tasting the word.

I stood. Leaning over the steps, I peeked in through the living room window. I could see clear back to the dining room, where Rev was hunched over his coffee, tapping his spoon against the saucer. He was singing some Bible song, I was sure.

I scooted back down, near Grandmother. I let Jerome's feet lay in my lap.

"Tell me a story."

Grandmother looked right, then left, up and down the street. No Block Party ghosts remained. Only a few folks like us, tired, and lingering, reluctant to recognize a new day.

Grandmother patted my arm. "There was a girl, as old as you, Jewell, child, who spread the word that a day that seemed an ordinary day—same sun, same sky, same street, same everything—was really a special day. Block Party Day. She skipped and sang and ate and played.

"She got all the folks to believe her—to set aside their cares—to celebrate. For the old to be young again. And for the young to shine brightest with the magic of youth. Like a Pied Piper. She lured them into being their innocent selves. Their best selves."

"But you told me to do it."

"Maybe so. But you made it happen. You have the touch,

magic, joy in your soul. It was your call they heeded. Not mine." She clasped my hand within hers.

I swelled with pride. Yes, I was just a child. But Grandmother made me feel powerful. I could feel joy . . . and I could make it!

A star shot across the sky.

What lesson was Grandmother teaching me? What was her porch story telling? I scrunched my nose.

Grandmother was telling me it was important to take joy, not just by yourself but with family, friends, community. Everyone can contribute to everyone else's joy.

Joy can be a shared gift.

Even a child can make hearts take wing.

You never need an excuse for joy.
Celebrate being alive.

"Don't call the dead if you aren't serious."

Grandmother's words were unexpected. We'd been sitting for a good half hour, quiet on the steps, enjoying a slight breeze of cool air. Clouds hung overhead, making the sky seem moonless and starless. There was a kaleidoscope of lights, flickering behind our neighbors' curtains. Inside houses, the play of shadows told puppet tales, while outside, others were nothing but shadows on false porches. Sometimes a cigarette tip would burn red in the dark. Or a pipe would shine a small bowl of embers. Mainly it was dark; and I was one of the few kids, unafraid. Even porch voices spoke in whispers.

I scratched a mosquito bite on my thigh.

"Did I ever tell you about the time your Aunt Hattie brought her momma back from the dead?" Grandmother's voice was dry.

"Naw. It's not possible."

"All things possible."

"With Jesus. Isn't that what you taught me?"

"Yes. But where you think our people come from? We go way back to roots, herbs, hoodoo, voodoo. To far, far away on an African shore. Christianity is but one kind of faith. For black peoples, yellow peoples, orange peoples, all kinds of peoples, there are other traditions too. All kinds of faiths preserve mysteries."

"Like 'Scratch a wall, somebody die.' "

"Yes."

" 'Burn the hair from your brush, for if a bird snatches it, uses it for its nest, your hair will fall right out.' "

"Yes."

" 'A broken-winged bird means trouble.' "

"Yes, trouble and sorrow."

" 'The world is full of signs.' "

"That's right, Jewell, girl. Dreams bear witness to our lives."

I let out a big whoosh. Grandmother was full of wonders. Unlike the night, she scared me some. For I felt her power, and sometimes she seemed larger than life, but then I'd blink and she'd just be Grandmother, tired from worry and chores. An ordinary woman. But, of course, she wasn't ordinary—no more than any grandmother is ordinary. She had wisdom, born deep from her experience.

"Some of this might seem like nonsense. But always remember, slaves weren't blank slates. They didn't just give up their African beliefs. When they were forbidden to praise their gods, their faith went underground. Blended with Christianity. You know how folks sing, in church?"

"Yes, ma'am."

"You know how they get the spirit and sometimes fall to the floor?"

"And the ushers have to catch them, fan them 'til they're better. Mrs. Watson does it all the time." I cringed, for I was embarrassed by short, squat Mrs. Watson's trembling, like she had some tic or fire ants in her pants. She'd sway, shout,

"Praise Jesus. Praise Jesus." Everybody would be watching her as she left her pew and seemed to skip up and down before the altar. She'd dance, clap her hands, and shout out to God. Before you knew it, and every time it seemed like a surprise, she'd just fall over. Like a marionette's strings getting cut. Most times, ushers were there to catch her. But once she fell and had a huge bump on the back of her head for days.

"Mrs. Watson is *feeling* what Africans believed. That only music could call spirits, encouraging possession. Maybe it's the Holy Ghost that rides her? 'Holy Ghost' is a Christian name. But Africans thought there were all kinds of spirits—gods of water, war, and earth. A god spirit for almost everything. Maybe the sea god is possessing her?"

"Like Poseidon?"

"Or maybe the goddess of love?"

"Like Venus?"

"Or Mary. Names don't matter. What matters is that Africans believed spirits could enter them, and as far as I know, anywhere that slaves practiced faith, music was important because music calls the gods, spirits, the Holy Ghost, whatever you want to call THEM or IT to enter a believer's soul."

I clasped my hands, muttering a quick prayer that one day

I'd feel the spirit inside me. So far, I'd just enjoyed singing gospel, being among other choir children. I didn't always listen well to Rev's sermons. I promised never to laugh or squirm because of Mrs. Watson again.

I touched Grandmother's knee. "So, what happened to Aunt Hattie?"

"Aunt Hattie was low on money. She thought if she could hit a number, she'd be able to catch up. Pay her rent. Maybe even buy a new dress."

"How'd she do it?"

"Call the dead? It's really simple, and I'm not going to tell you the whole truth, else you'll try it."

I grinned silly.

"Curiosity killed the cat."

"I'm no cat."

"A kitten, maybe."

"Gram!"

"Nonetheless, I mean it, Jewell, girl. Even grown folks like Hattie get into trouble. Calling the dead is serious."

"But how? Do you do a dance?"

"Simple, really. You put the name of your ancestor and the contents of your wish under your pillow. Then, you put a glass of water under the bed, under the pillow, under your sleepy head."

"What's the water for?"

"Two things. It's easier for spirits to move through water. Connect from their world to ours. When they arrive, they're thirsty. So, a glass of water is plain good manners."

"Then what?"

"That's what I'm not going to tell you. It's important that you say some words."

"From the Bible?"

"Some. But they're also from long ago. Like the words the slaves misremembered, didn't remember. Come from our African souls."

Why tell me all this now? It was just another too-hot night. Way past midnight. Not enough time to wheedle more information from Grandmother. My dad had already crawled into bed. Tonie and Aleta were inside sucking on oranges, watching *Topper*. Grandpa was dozing in the dining room chair, hunched over his bitter coffee.

Grandma looked at the sky. "The stars are miracles. Part of God's alphabet."

"Stars mean something?"

"You bet. Ancients been reading them for forever. Slaves read them too. See the big dipper there?"

I squinted.

"Pretend you're connecting dots. You see a big dipper, then a smaller one."

"My, I do." I felt awestruck.

"Follow the drinking gourds. That's another name for the Big and Little Dippers. One star, in the handle of the Little Dipper, is the North Star. Slaves used it to guide themselves to freedom."

"What about Aunt Hattie?"

"I'm telling you. Connect the dots, Jewell, girl."

"They don't make sense."

"Pay attention. Did you know down South everybody cherishes dreams? In dreams this world and the next mix like sugar and grits.

"Aunt Hattie put a glass of water under her bed, right beneath her pillow, quoted from the Bible, and chanted some slave prayer. She took a slip of paper and wrote, 'Give me a number,' then she slipped it on top of the water glass and slept."

"She dreamed it all," I shrilled with understanding.

"No, this world and the next mixed. She called her momma back. Her momma gave her the number 337. Then she slapped her. Full on the cheek, saying, 'Never call me back for such nonsense again.'

"In the morning, Aunt Hattie ran to the numbers runner to place her bet. Folks in the barbershop stared. Aunt Hattie felt like her slip was showing, or her dress wasn't buttoned up. Finally, the barber asked, 'What happened to your face?'

" 'What you mean?'

"Hattie looked in the mirror and saw her mother's handprint on her face. Saw a deep black, kind of burnt flesh that marked her."

I shivered.

"She ran home and didn't come out for half a year until her mark faded. Faded, but never left."

"Did her number hit?"

"Of course it did. But that's not the point. You can call the dead. The dead are with us everywhere. Every good-bye ain't gone."

Grandmother took my hand, pushed it into the night air. "Feel it?"

"Naw."

"As you grow, you will. The very air is alive with spirits. From long ago. Or from yesterday."

"Don't they"—I looked about, squinting, trying to see between air—"go to heaven?"

"Sure they do. But it doesn't mean they're gone. They're elsewhere and can travel when they choose. Like guardians. See that tree? It's alive. The stars, moon . . . even this road has tales to tale. The universe is alive. Everything. There is no end. Respect the world around you, Jewell, girl. Respect the dead, for they ain't gone."

"If you die, will you be gone?"

"Never."

"Can I call on you?'

"Sure thing, baby. All the time. I'll probably be walking beside you most times. Or else watching you from on high. But don't call me back and ask me to make my self visible for foolishness, for money. You're meant to live your life well—call when things are most bleak. For your soul, not money or things.

"Calling the dead is serious. But every life in this world goes on. Every life signifies. And when you need help, call on

God, but every person that's ever lived is part of you—an ancestor. All good spirits are ready to help."

"And the bad spirits? Are they in hell?"

"Yes. But they wander too, whispering foolishness in weak people's ears. Causing harm."

"But you won't let them harm me?" I looked up into her face. High cheekbones. Wide eyes and a wide mouth. The only face of a mother/grandmother I'd ever known. Could ever remember.

"Call me. I'll always be near."

"Promise?"

"Promise."

Like an invisible telephone, I thought. I'd talk with Grandmother as long as she was alive and beyond.

A year later, I learned the truth of Grandmother's porch story. I was in bed (a school night, not a summer's night) and restless, for a thunderstorm racked the sky. No rain—just noise—and, in the dark, my riding horse seemed to shudder on its wire rings. I heard Grandmother rise from bed, but it was too early to be rising for laundry and chores. Grandmother walked, no, truly floated past my bedroom door. Tonie and Aleta didn't stir. I swung my feet to the cold floor, peeked round the door, and watched as Grandmother walked down three flights of stairs and sat at the telephone stand in the hall. She picked up the phone though it didn't ring, and I heard her say, "Yes, yes." Then she hung up and climbed the stairs. I scooted into bed and raised the covers to shield my face.

Grandmother was opening the closet in the room beside ours. "What are you doing, woman?" I heard Rev ask. "What are you doing?" Grandmother didn't answer, or if she did, it was too low for me to hear.

The phone rang, loud and wailing. Over and over. Rev was in his long johns, getting ready to climb down the stairs, when Grandmother, all dressed, her best coat on, passed him (Rev, openmouthed) and went and lifted the phone. "Yes, yes," she said. "I know and I'm ready."

"Woman, what is wrong with you?" Rev shouted. By this time, even my Pop was leaning his head over the second banister and the boys were poking their heads through banister bars. Tonie stole behind me. Aleta didn't stir.

"Aunt Hattie died. 'Bout an hour ago. Ernie's coming to pick me up."

"But you're already dressed, Momma? How could that be?" shouted Pop in jeans and bare feet.

Grandmother looked down at herself. "So I am." Then she looked up at all of our awestruck faces just as another thunder crack rattled the sky.

"Hattie called. Told me she was dead."

Nobody believed her, or if they did, they didn't say so that night. Rev got dressed and clutched his Bible. Pop looked after the boys and Tonie. They were scared. "From thunder," they said, lying.

After Ernie, Grandmother, and Rev left to take care of Aunt Hattie's body, I stole downstairs in my slippered feet and sat at the telephone stand, waiting for Aunt Hattie to call me. Not expecting the phone to ring, I lifted the receiver every five minutes, knowing that any second, I might hear a voice: "Jewell, is that you? Jewell?" instead of static.

When your soul aches, speak to the dead.
Ancestors who loved you, still do.

They're always listening.
If you let yourself hear, they'll guide you.

"Be thankful."

W hat?" I was itching like ants were in my pants, playing football on my arms. It was my sister's fault.

"Jewell, let's garden," she'd said, and I'd been delighted
that my older sister had wanted to do something with me. I'd
puffed my chest out and said, "Sure."

We didn't garden in Grandma's tiny yard. Instead, we went
two blocks over to a vacant lot with scarred tires that toughs
had set ablaze. True, dozens of black-eyed Susans opened their
faces to the sun, but most of the lot was weeds, brush, and
empty cans of Iron City or Rolling Rock beer. Even though I
had doubts, I plucked right in when my sister said, "Dig" or

"Pull." Even after ten minutes, the dirt square was still untilled and a downright mess, but I'd begun to itch. Shamefully. Hopping like a jumping bean; my sister, who'd been serious, dictatorial, started squealing. Laughing at me, yelling, "Poison. Poison ivy."

I wailed all the way home.

Tonie got sent to bed even though the sun was midsky. I got calamine lotion (I looked like a pink little pig!) and Grandmother cooing all over me. She even fried my favorite—pork chops—and didn't make me eat my brussels sprouts. Still, I was fuming. I thought of a dozen ways to pay my sister back. I'd cut her pigtails off when she slept. I'd hide her best dress. Pour molasses in her underwear drawer. Scratch her favorite 45s—"My Guy" and "My Girl." Icky-stuff. But I'd do none of those things, having learned that the high road was if not a key to godliness, then an opportunity to avoid a spanking while having the moral upper hand against my sister. No wonder she sometimes hated me.

I liked being the tortured saint. Suffering was my art. And if I was scooting, squirming a bit too much, complaining a bit too loudly, no one knew it but me. Or so I thought.

Grandmothers know everything.

"Be thankful."

"I am."

"Truly?"

Grandmother was looking at me. "Okay," I said. "I forgive her."

"What?"

"My sister. I forgive her."

"Aren't you nice."

"Gram!"

"Jewell, child!" Grandmother fussed right back. "Just be— that's all she wants. Be thankful. Be kind. Be nice."

"But I am."

"Always?"

Course not. I sighed with all my best drama. "But neither is she."

" 'Course not. We're all human. We all make mistakes. Just be."

"What's that mean?"

"It means not embarrassing your sister in front of her friends."

It was times like this that I swore Grandmother was "omnipotent," with big eyes in the back of her head. "Like

God," they'd explained in Sunday school. "Omnipotent is God."

Except God never talked back to me and told me my sins. Grandma did.

How'd she know that I'd read my sister's lovesick diary? How'd she know that I'd read it to her friends? At a neighbor's house! How'd she know that Tonie had chased me until, winded, she'd just plopped down and cried? How'd she know that even though I'd known I should have said sorry, I hadn't. Worse, I hadn't even felt bad when I hadn't said sorry.

I was more than sorry now. I felt like an earthworm, deserving to be squashed! I'd left my moral high ground and become depraved. Tempted once and for all to get the better of my older sister, I'd been criminal.

Worse, I knew my sister hadn't told Grandmother. Tonie wasn't a snitch.

Skin itching, feeling hotter by the minute, I felt ashamed. I scooted my butt forward on the cold step and made to rise. Gram's hand on my elbow stopped me. "You can say you're sorry later. I want to talk with you now." Her voice was flat.

I sat back down, ready to accept more scolding. But silence stretched like an endless rubber band. I clasped my hands together to keep from scratching. A breeze skittered a twig down the street. There was a low murmur from other steps. Darkened shadows stood, sat, moved like ghosts, ancestral spirits. A screen door slammed, letting a flash of light knife into the quiet black. No one had porch lights. Just the glow from streetlamps high overhead, the spilling glare from TVs, windows, and doors interrupted our late-night, outdoor living room.

I was getting scared, for I thought surely Grandmother was truly mad at me. I, the "good" girl, had been "bad." Mean-spirited.

"Did I ever tell you 'bout my favorite holiday?"

I scratched my neck.

Grandmother snatched my hand down. "Don't go near your face. You don't want scars, do you?"

"No, m'am," I mumbled, still bewildered by Grand-mother's "holiday."

"Did I?"

"What?"

"Tell you about my favorite holiday?"

"Naw."

"Can you guess?"

"Christmas?"

"No." Grandmother smiled.

"That's my favorite. Christmas. This year I want a Party Barbie—"

Grandmother glared at me.

"Easter?" I squeaked.

"No. Though I'm grateful for spring and Christ's resurrection."

"Juneteenth?" I asked with a squirt of joy. "When slaves heard they were free?"

"No." Grandmother's face relaxed, making her more beautiful. "Thanksgiving."

"Seems like nothing but work to me." Like a picture book, I could see flashes of Grandmother, days before Thanksgiving, dusting like crazy, polishing dishes, soaking, bending, lifting loads of laundry, ironing napkins and the fancy tablecloth, putting fresh linens on cots for relatives. Plus, she did all the considerable work she normally did—getting us kids breakfast, lunch boxes, and snacks. (Even made cupcakes for the school play.) Then, sweaty in the kitchen, after having already fixed the evening meal, she'd be opening cans of preserves, dumping them into ready-made pie crusts. All the while Grandmother's face was anxious and tight, her back, feet, and hands aching, and all the time grumbling because she didn't have her own preserves, set down months ago, didn't have time to make a half dozen crusts fresh. Or dry bread for her famous sage and sausage stuffing. Or make squash soup and pumpkin filling from scratch. Or shape butter into turkey molds. But she never compromised her biscuits. Letting flour and water slowly rise, then beating it down, letting it rise again and again. Then, kneading, rolling out dough. Her pride and joy. Air biscuits. So light they'd float if given half a chance.

Me, my sister, and Aleta peeled potatoes, but with more skins hitting the floor than the bags, I wondered if Grandmother was just keeping us busy. (It was the only time she smiled—slicing celery and mushrooms as we kids gouged the potatoes that she'd turn into a silken mash.) Frantic, frenetic, Grandmother washed and dried the turkey, bigger than a toddler, basting it every twenty minutes, all night until sunrise on Thanksgiving Day. Giblet gravy bubbled in a saucepan, green beans brightened over steaming water, the oven hissed on and off, keeping a steady 350 degrees, making the house humid with heat while wind rattled outside.

Thanksgiving afternoon, grown-ups, like buzzards,

swooped, devouring in a few hours all that food cooked for days. Half the folks I didn't know. They were "blood-relatives," but, for some of them, I thought, the blood gave out a long time ago. One foot was definitely in the grave. A great-uncle had two feet. The men, loud, guzzling beer, watched football. The women did dishes. But it seemed to me that many just kept drying the same old plate and Grandmother was definitely left scouring the pots. The children who could walk were told to go outside and play, whether we wanted to or not.

I was not a fan of turkey day.

"Down South—"

The magic words. "Oh," I exhaled. I forgot my itching; my skin started tingling in a new way.

"My Momma . . ." Grandmother leaned forward, squinting at me. "I told you about her?"

"Some."

"Down South, mommas were sometimes too strict. Too rigid. Too know-it-all about everybody else's business. They had to be. Down South, when I was growing up, life was dangerous. Segregated. One person's actions could threaten a whole community. One person's actions could get their selves killed."

"Like Emmett Till?" I'd seen his bloated, battered body in *Jet*. The magazine came each month, and every year they wrote about the anniversary of his death. The year always haunted me—1954. Emmett Till died the year I was born.

"Yes, like Emmett Till and even worse before that." Grandmother patted her chest, the way she sometimes did in church, and gave out a holler: "Praise be.

"Down South, Momma was, in some ways, like all the other mommas. She had her disagreements with my dad, her sisters. Everybody. There was a right way and a wrong way to do everything."

I blinked.

"I'm not criticizing. Momma would often say the same about herself. She'd say. 'Important to know yourself. Know your limitations.' *Li-mi-ta-tions*. That word would roll off her tongue. 'We're all flawed, she'd say.' "

"You're not." I smiled, thinking she'd wrap me in her arms; instead, I was alarmed when Grandmother drew back.

"Oh, yes, I am. And I'm proud to be. Flawed. This world ain't 'bout perfection. It's about striving—that's what's good—being imperfect, yet striving to be perfect and loving yourself despite your flaws."

"I don't get it."

"My momma did. And of all the times she was most imperfect and perfect both, it was during the month of November."

Grandmother peered into the night like she could see what no one else could. Her eyes were fixed, didn't blink. She pursed her lips.

"One October 31, we—me, my sisters, and brothers—all decided to be ghosts. Cutting out eyes in old sheets. Running like demons through the pecan trees. Sheets billowing too-too white in the moonlight.

"Momma saw us from the kitchen window. She slammed open the screen and stomped outside, clutching at my brother first. 'Take this off.' Pulling so hard at the sheet that it snapped. Pulling so hard, she yanked both hair and cotton. Pulling so hard, her hands felt like the wrath of a stranger. One by one, she kept screaming, 'Take it off.' Snatching, frightening us with her grim, flailing determination. All us kids came together, watching her tearing at them white sheets. She couldn't seem to catch a breath, couldn't seem to get a word out. She just spun round, headed back toward the house.

" 'Klan,' my older brother said. And I understood then

why Momma had been more terrified of us, romping in the darkness, than any Halloween ghost.

"November first, Momma woke us with a smile. The day before was a fading memory.

" 'Time to prepare,' she said. The boys had regular chores with Pop, but 'preparing' for Thanksgiving was our duty as girls.

" 'A little bit of work each day until Thanksgiving, and we'll have a fine feast,' Momma said.

"But it wasn't only about the day, it was about the process, all the steps in between. Momma set us down with a calendar, and for each day's square, she'd make a note: check preserves; churn butter; feed turkey more; shine dishes; order flour, candles, taffy; pick pecans; check table linens; feed turkey more . . . on and on it went. Some squares were so filled you couldn't read the numbers. Items repeated: polish silver, buff china; weed garden; water pumpkins, squash, and sweet potatoes; feed turkey more.

"It wasn't just about the day, but about the marking of time . . . of us, *being* together. Just as the moon waxed and waned, as nights grew colder and threatened frost, as fall prepared for winter, as the turkey was finally brought to slaughter,

Momma was preaching to us about seasons . . . about the rhythm of life, about the great pleasure to be found in domestic arts. Preparing this holiday was her time to shine, her time to pass all her considerable skills about cleaning, cooking, nurturing a family, creating a splendid day of thanksgiving—not just for the food on the table but for the gift of time, the gift of life—down to her children, across the generations.

"Understand?"

If I said yes, the story would end. So I shook my head no. Grandmother sighed. "Maybe we should go to bed."

"No, Grandmother, no. Tell me more. Please. I'll understand."

Grandmother's gnarled fingers traced the cracks on our steps. She looked about to cry.

"Momma taught us how to make beauty. The smell of beeswax and lemon. Boiling water with nutmeg and cinnamon sticks tossed in to simmer on the stove and make the house a dream. Linen sprayed with honeysuckle. Touch. The soft texture of fine, bright white linens covering the table, touching our mouths. The glory of dried corn, golden and red leaves, baby pumpkins making a fall centerpiece. We painted mason jars to hold flickering candles. I always painted mine with rainbows.

"We set aside smooth and rough seeds for next year's garden: broccoli, sweet potatoes, winter kale.

"Momma taught us that loving was shown through acts of time. Day in, day out. Loving was shown through nurturing her family. 'Men do it too, but different. Pop would plow fast, milk fast, right the fence fast,' said Momma. 'Women indulge time. Gentle seasons, seasonings. No shame in taking time; no care just for getting things done; just care for each step by step by step.'

"I loved making Thanksgiving, making our house lovely. I loved picking what turkey to put down . . . to turn into a family feast.

"I loved my power as a girl-child."

I touched Grandmother's hand. "I like our house just fine," I said. It wasn't true. Our house was a real mess, us kids not helping enough, our parents and grandfather too tired to help after a long day's work. Sometimes, I couldn't help wishing for a pretty house like Dick and Jane's. Neat crayon colors. Everything in its place within the lines.

Grandmother bowed her head. "I can't do as my momma did. I try. But I'm too imperfect."

"Trying is the main thing, right?" I wasn't certain that was the answer or not. But it *felt, sounded* right. Sounded like the lesson Grandmother was teaching me.

"Momma would always pat my hand. Say I did good even when I didn't. She taught me how to show thanks."

Grandmother pressed her fingers to her eyes.

"That fall, after our ghost haunting, I'd turned twelve. I'd stopped going to school. Momma was my only teacher. For her day, she was the best. Still—"

I laid my head in Grandmother's lap.

"—Momma was teaching me how to be a woman.

"Two days before Thanksgiving, Momma's calendar squares were so filled, no one could understand the squiggly marks but her.

"I woke with an ache in my lower back. We were at breakfast, adding butter and sugar to grits. There was a chill in the air and a cool wind drifting across the porch, against and through our kitchen window.

"My sister noticed blood on the chair. I jumped up, terrified. My sisters started wailing, and Momma shooed them out. Told them to help the boys. 'Help your Pop, she said.' Even though they hated boy chores, off they went like sad rabbits.

"Momma stopped everything. Stopped Thanksgiving preparations and turned all her energy to me. 'You a woman now,' she grinned, her arms akimbo. Then she kissed me on the tip of my nose.

"My fear turned to pride.

"Momma heated pots of water on the stove, pulled the big tin tub from the closet, and told me to undress and step inside. She mixed hot water with cold until it showered like a warm river down my body. Knobbly shoulders, small breasts, skinny legs, my scratched-up knees, my big feet. When the water was high enough, Momma told me to sit. 'Let the water soothe between your legs.' She scrubbed my back, washed my hair, then dried and oiled me like I was still a baby. She pointed at my thin strands of pubic hair.

" 'That's your sugar bush—where pleasure and life come together. Keep it safe. Share yourself with love and pride. Share yourself with your beloved.'

" 'Like you do with Pop?' "

" 'Hun-hunh,' she smiled sweetly. 'Never feel shame. You be a child of Eve.

" 'Your body has a gate. The first time, when it's still brand new, it can be a bit stiff . . . but once opened, your body will warm and open like petals on a flower. You are Nature's child. God's child.'

"She brushed my hair, slipped a fresh dress over my head and shoulders. Then, she showed me how to shape and stuff cotton squares between my thighs to catch my blood.

" 'Bleeding is part of your life's season. One day, you'll be a mother. Teaching. Loving. Praise be. Just be. For all this, be thankful. This is truly the best Thanksgiving.'

"She brought me tea and biscuits. Placed a heated quilt pad behind my back, let me sit like a queen, most of the day feeling the stiff pad between my legs soften with blood.

"She stopped all her cooking. Just kept me company in the kitchen with light streaming through the windows, making crystals on the floor. She put dried marigolds on the table before me (did you know marigolds are Mary's flower, God's mother's favorite bloom?), and she knitted, hummed, sang, and asked if I wanted more tea.

"I felt so good. Precious. My body's calendar was more important than the days or weeks of holiday preparations. I was the *good news* celebration.

"Come afternoon, Momma said, 'Let me show you how to bury your blood's seeds.'

"She handed me another linen pad, helped me unpin the old one and fold it into tighter and tighter squares. Then she taught me to tie another cloth around the red bloom.

" 'Come,' she said, and we went outside to bury my flowering in dirt. Momma believed in 'old-school ways'—burying umbilical cords, cauls, a woman's blood. She dug a hole with the spade. 'Your mound is right beside mine. The two of them will nourish the soil. Nurture new growth.' She scattered leaves on top of my slight mound.

" 'Never feel wanting. Just be.' Momma cried; she was so happy for me. So happy we were women together, growing strong, carrying on an ancient line. That was my favorite holiday. My finest Thanksgiving."

Grandmother was crying, letting big drops stream down her chin. She clutched my hand, and I felt as if she'd break it.

"Jewell, child, think always of your outrageous glory. You're a month of Sundays. A dozen years of thanksgiving.

"One day you'll be a woman true. Connected to mother earth—the big blue world—the robins, sky, mountains, dirt.

"The meaning of Thanksgiving will be you. Every twenty-eight days, until you're creating a child, your body will mimic the seasons. Give thanks.

"Shine. Like me. Like your sisters. Your grandmothers. Like all the women of this whole wide world."

I sniffed, feeling a sweet melancholy. *Where would my momma be when my blood fell down?*

"That evening," Grandmother went on, "we all said dinner table prayers. Poppa treated me with a new kind of deference. My sisters seemed younger; my brothers, from another world.

"That evening, I became Momma's right-hand woman. I helped put the kids to bed. I did the dishes, added lemon juice to the fruit pies. The next day, for the first time, Momma let me baste the turkey. Thanksgiving Day, she let me lay it down before Poppa while the kids 'aaahed' and 'ooohed.'

"Jewell, child, Thanskgiving ain't just about Indians feeding Puritans. Thanksgiving is the power of creation—sowing seeds, reaping harvests for your family, your community, and within yourself. Creation is in every woman's hands, heart. The world is our home. Time can be slowed."

"Like now?"

"You bet."

"And when there isn't enough time?"

"You take shortcuts, like I need to do. But Jewell child, if your body started flowing today, I'd stop everything and make sure you knew that touching, cleaning, oiling you was a part of life's process and celebration. Nothing like a woman's first time to holler, 'Praise be.' 'Bear witness.' Be Thankful. Just be. There is no greater glory."

My flow wouldn't come for years, but I wished that when it did, my Grandmother would be there to care for me.

I wanted my ritual of pride. My sense that I was my own Thanksgiving.

"Just be," Grandmother said.

"Just be," I echoed.

"Your being connects you to women since the dawn of time. So?"

I squinted. "So. I should be kind to my sister."

"That's right. She'll become a woman soon. Before you. She'll help be your guide. Love her. A woman needs her sister."

I stood, ready to climb the modest outdoor stairs, then the three flights inside. "I'll tell her sorry."

"And that you'll be kinder? Nicer?"

"Sure will."

"What if I'm not there when your time comes?"

I pretended not to hear. The double doors both swung shut. I double-timed it up the stairs.

The room was dark. My sister wasn't sleeping. I could tell because she was lying flat on her back. Aleta was snoring; the plastic rocking horse with creaking, metal hinges seemed ominous. I stood over my sister on her bed and said, "I'm sorry. Double, triple sorry."

"I'm sorry too."

"Don't you like me?"

"Sure, I do. But I don't want you to share my secrets."

"Right. I'm sorry."

I put on my flannel gown and dived into the bed next to my sis. Grandmother was right, her blood would flow before mine.

"When we make Thanksgiving, I think we ought to do without turkey. Have ham instead. And only apple pies."

"No pumpkin?"

"Only if you really want. Grandmother says you'll be my only sister. We should stay close."

Tonie put out her hand. My hand met hers above the river of wood between our two beds. My pinky wrapped around hers, then her index finger touched mine, then our hands clasped tightly. Sister-to-sister. Soon to be women together. Forever.

Love yourself despite and because of
your flaws. Strive to be better.

Every woman is your sister.

Celebrate a woman's power for creation.

*"The best stew is a mixed-blood stew.
Just like with a real stew, you need
pepper and salt, all kinds of vegetables
bubbling in the pot."*

P lease, Grandma, I'm tired." I was propped up in bed
with three pillows.

"You don't want to hear a story?"

"No," I murmured, tears welling.

"Don't cry. You'll make the bandage itch."

"I don't care." But I did care. I wanted to stop feeling so miserable. It was August. Summer was coming to a close and I could barely move. Run, jump, and play was out of the question. I'd been hit by a car. My head and face were bandaged, and only my nose, mouth, and one eye peeped through. I had bruises everywhere; scabs made a crooked path down my arms and right leg.

Me, Aleta, and Tonie had been crossing our street with Mrs. Chalmers's eldest daughter, Kim, who'd been telling us, "Go!" She'd yelled and I'd dashed out. I hadn't heard her say, "Stop. Wait. Get back."

I didn't remember the ambulance ride. Or the hospital stay. Or even the ride back home. Pop told me he'd held me, cradled in his arms, and Rev had driven "ever so slowly" so no bump could cause me pain.

I only remembered waking up in bed, feeling more pain than I'd ever had, and feeling petrified. Sorry for myself. The first word I hollered was "Ma," but there wasn't any mother to hold my hand, feed me soup, give me aspirin, and make me laugh as I felt stranded in our top-floor room while the house below was alive and my sister and cousins and all the kids were outside, hollering and singing and having the time of their lives.

"What color are black people?" asked Grandmother.

"I don't know." It was daytime, we weren't on the porch, and Grandmother had loads of laundry to do.

"We are our own special rainbow. Red-toned Mrs. Chalmers, sandy-faced Willie, beyond-midnight Rev, and ivory-skinned Mrs. Jackson. Chocolate. Coffee. Café au lait.

High yellow. Indigo. Bronze. Sepia girls. Every one of us beautiful."

"So?"

"Your momma didn't believe that."

I perked up, even though an inch forward made me hurt. No one talked about my mother. It was more like she was dead rather than left, gone, walked off without a fare-thee-well.

Grandmother's face looked sorrowful. Lines seemed deeper, etched in around her eyes and mouth. Unlike the porch stories, she wasn't happy telling me about my mother. Just as I knew she wasn't happy that I'd been hit by a car.

My first night home, I was groggy and couldn't open my eyes. Grandmother and Pop thought I was sleeping. Grandmother kept repeating, "I should've been there. Been watching them. I should've walked them across the street." Nothing Pop said seemed to soothe her.

"Please, Grandmother. Go on. I'll listen."

She clutched my hand. "Times are going to be hard. Life's hard. To make it, you've got to love who you be. Always.

"Your momma was a beautiful woman. High yellow, men always fell at her feet. Including your father. They made your sister, Tonie, before they were married."

"Oooo," I cooed. I didn't know the details, just basic principles. Boy+Girl=Baby.

"It's all right. They did marry. But, except for having you, perhaps they should have gone their separate ways."

"What's that got to do with rainbow colors?"

Sun was streaming, making my rocking horse by the window glisten. He seemed to be inviting me to ride away. If I'd felt better, I would've. Listening to Grandmother felt like swallowing cod liver oil. Her words were good for me, but I didn't like what I was hearing.

"Your momma didn't like how she got her color. High yellow. Didn't like the fact that you could trace somewhere in her blood a Master's white blood. You understand me?"

"Like a Master was somebody's father?"

"Yes. And not by marriage. Since slavery and a long time afterwards, it's been illegal for a white man or woman to marry a black.

"Your mother carried a deep shame, and since she wasn't light enough to pass, she chose to leave the folks that knew her and make a new life story for herself. She got caught up trying to make a white life rather than a human one."

"I don't understand."

"Didn't think you would, at least not right away."

I could tell Grandmother wanted to hold me, but there wasn't any place free of pain on my body. So she patted the bed. "You want a popsicle?"

"Banana?"

"You bet." Grandmother shuffled down the stairs, and I stared at my arms and hands, at the veins popping up and winding like a crazy quilt in my body. Since I was light brown, that meant there was white blood in me too. But why should I mind? Like my momma did? Did it matter? When I looked in the mirror I saw me. Jewell. Before the bandages you could see the freckles arching over my nose. See dark eyes and brown skin.

I scratched at the bandage over my right eye, wondering if it would ever see again. Doctor said we'd know in six weeks when he unwrapped the bandages.

"Here goes." Grandmother split the popsicle in two. One banana ice stick for me; the other, for her.

"White folks used to say one drop of black blood makes you a slave. Made it a law too. Sheer foolishness. Pepper in the pot makes everything taste better. Can't use just salt."

"You're saying I'm a stew?"

"Yes. The best kind. Mixed-blood stew. You remember last summer when we went down South?"

Did I ever. I hated every minute of the ride. Rev drove like crazy, without stopping. Fourteen hours. Drinking thermos after thermos of mud coffee to keep him awake. Only after we pleaded and whined did he let us pee in the fields. Driving South, beyond the Mason-Dixon Line, Rev didn't want to meet no cops. When we pleaded for food other than our bologna sandwiches, he said no. "Everything is segregated down here."

"Toilets too?"

Rev's bushy brows pinched together in the rearview mirror. "Toilets too," he said. "Best thing is to keep moving."

So we did . . . keep moving, driving to Grandmother's parents' home—exhausted, bladders full, and thrilled to fall out of the car.

But the trip was worth it. To see such a big white house with a porch as wide as our street—it was amazing. A wrap-around porch with rockers, a swing, and small tables to put down drinks or hold a checkerboard. You could have a party on the porch. Invite the whole neighborhood for lemonade and tea.

And just beyond the porch was more nature than I'd ever seen: trees, flowers, bushes, butterflies, fireflies, bluebirds, ants, and squirrels. Dozens of crows.

It was paradise for us kids. A month of revelations. A whole month of clear air, growing things, and more relatives than we could count.

I remember glimpsing my great-grandmother, half Seminole and half black, sitting in her bed (like I'm sitting now) wearing a white flannel gown. She was so frail I thought she was a ghost. So silent, I thought her mute.

I stood in the doorway watching her brush, over and over again, her long strands of black silk. Hair was so long she could sit on it. Hair so dark it gleamed like polished rock.

For three days I watched her with each setting sun. Finally, I asked, "Why does she do it, Grandmother? What for?"

"She's afraid water will make her catch cold. So she brushes away the dirt. Stroke by stroke."

I remember thinking, *No more shampoos and hot combs for me!*

But Grandmother snapped, "Don't you think it!"

I dreaded the iron comb pressing my kinky hair flat.

Grandfather, who never told porch stories, told them down

South. In Pittsburgh, when he wasn't in the pulpit, he mainly grunted. Snarled, "Be good. Stop running" when we kids raced by.

That evening, not even minding the mosquitoes, I whispered to Rev, "I got Seminole in me."

"Seminole be all right," he growled. "But I got Choctaw and Irish in me." Rev lit a pipe like he was "King of the Mountain." He looked right at me. Clear, direct, like he was sharing thoughts with me just like he would with a grown-up.

"In the twenties, Irish come to the Pittsburgh steel mills. Stood the heat 'like niggers,' some say. I say they stood the heat like men who appreciated an extra dollar at the end of the day." He jabbed his pipe. "Negroes got fifty cents.

"My Irish grand-dad, nearly bald, freckled all over, fell in love with my grandmother, who had some white in her from a generation before. She had Choctaw too. Warrior blood. My grandmother's mama already had several of Master's children. One year, to spite him, she got pregnant by an Indian. Master was fit to be tied."

"So what all that blood makes me?"

Rev laughed, his mouth wide like a neighing horse. "Well, true to tell, remember I'm just your step-grandpa. I love you for forgetting that. But I do know," he looked up at Grandmother, "that you might have some Irish in you. Or maybe it's English? That's where your freckles come from."

I touched my blushing face.

He spoke in his pulpit voice, loud enough for the owls to hear. "I can tell you what all that mixed blood makes of me. Makes of you." He leaned real close. I could see tiny hairs growing on his lip. "Someone smart. Someone with the best of the best."

"Oh," I exhaled, while Rev slapped his leg, his laughter ending in a fit of coughing.

Grandmother gave me a napkin to wipe the popsicle juice from my mouth. "Down South, you saw some of your heritage: Indian and black. It's time to see more." She slipped her hand in her housedress's deep pocket and pulled out a folded obituary torn from the newspaper.

"That's your father's daddy," said Grandmother, handing me the newsprint.

"That's Grandfather Thornton?"

"No. I was married before. This is your father's daddy."

"He's white."

"He's dead."

A sad-eyed man seemed to stare right through me. He was in a naval uniform, handsome with a high forehead like mine and with a squared-off chin like Daddy's. Name given: Lieutenant J. Parker. Bold headline read: SERVED VALIANTLY IN THE WAR. Plain print: SURVIVED BY HIS WIFE AND FOUR KIDS.

"My grandfather's white?"

"Or else so light he passed. It wasn't clear. One time, he told me he was French Canadian. Another time, Irish. Another time, he said he was colored. Another time, Southern white."

My heart skipped, excited by this odd revelation.

"Why you stopped being married to him? The other man?"

"In a way, I didn't. He left. Said a sailor couldn't be an officer unless he be white. So, he chose white."

"He passed?"

"Maybe."

"Did you divorce him?"

"Didn't have the money. I had two kids to raise. Your

grandfather, the real one, Reverend Thornton and I jumped the broom."

I puffed my cheeks out. This was better than the movies. "This other grandfather, did he marry? Was his other wife white?"

"Yes. And his kids, all white. Or, at least, so they think. They live about thirty miles from here."

"No lie."

"Watch your mouth."

"I'm sorry."

Grandmother paused. She held my hand. "The white Parkers don't want to know you," she said flatly. "You understand?"

I tried to imagine the white Parkers who'd never lay claim to me or my father.

In my mind's eye, I could see Pop, dressed in his good pants and shirt, going to court to prove he was Lt. Parker's eldest son. "He wanted the flag from his father's military coffin," Grandmother said. "He wanted his white brothers and sisters to see and acknowledge him. They never did."

"See here," said Grandmother. "Read."

I tilted my head toward my good eye and read the obituary's bottom line. "Died of liver failure."

"Means he drank himself to death."

I don't know why, but I cried, not caring about my bandaged eye. All I wanted was my mother. A woman I'd never seen, never even remembered. I thought if she was here, life would be better. I wouldn't have been hit by a car. Wouldn't have felt so lonely and woebegone in the house. Wouldn't be listening to sad stories about my mother leaving, my grandfather dying.

"Jewell, child. Color and race in America is crazy. You're a mixed-blood stew. That's a wonderful thing. You've got to love yourself, all people, brown or otherwise. All blood runs red."

"So my mother isn't here because of me. I mean, she liked me. Didn't she?"

"Of course she did. But she's like my first husband. Prejudiced against her own people. Against her self.

"We are a new people. Descendents of slaves, mixed with the blood of white masters. Mixed with Indian. Irish. Italian. Maybe even some Polish. Who knows? We are a crazy quilt of blood—us. Coloreds. Black folks. But as a people, we stick together. Just as we open our hearts to others of all races. All blood runs red. Christian charity. Christian love. It's African too. 'Love and respect all things—alive or dead.' Understand?"

"I think so." I scratched the bandage over my blind eye. Grandmother pulled my hand down.

"I'm sorry your mother isn't here. I'm sorry I couldn't keep the car from hitting you. I'm sorry. Sometimes those you love, those you need, aren't going to be around when you need them most."

I was bawling full out. Grandmother hugged me, her hands light on my back.

"You've got to do what you did, Jewell. Survive. Fight on through. You're healing. Your body is healing itself. I'm proud of you for being strong."

That last August, before I went into second grade, I thought about loving all the blood, all the heritages inside me. I was an African American, a mixed-blood, powerful stew. I was strong.

In third grade, my mother came to claim me and took my sister and me to California. I didn't want to go, but since she and my father were trying marriage one more time, I had little choice. We were the only African American family in a suburban white community. The community was fine. But Mother, unfortunately, was skittish that we'd seem too rowdy—which meant, in her mind, too colored. The first night, she laid down rules, soft yet insistent commands about propriety, about being pretty in a dull, not flamboyant, way. "Be charming. Be gracious," she said.

At fifteen, I'd grown rebellious. Become a hippie and a power-to-the-people child. "Times they are a'changing . . . Say it loud, I'm black and I'm proud."

I painted my bedroom red and black and hung fishnets from the ceiling. African spears and masks were propped on the wall. A strobe light flickered in the corner, making every movement seem like two. Jimi Hendrix and the Jefferson Airplane blared from my stereo. I was celebrating my bloodlines and, for me, a black flower child was not a contradiction. I wore a bushy Afro and leopard prints with love beads and a lei of flowers. My Huey Newton print scared Mother more than the possibility of me burning down the house, trying to light incense.

My support of the Olympians' black power salute frightened her more than the potential of me doing hard drugs at a pool party in a neighbor's backyard.

Mother kicked me out of the house. "Go," she said; Pop said nothing. I flew from California back to Pittsburgh, to my birthplace, to Grandmother and Rev.

Grandmother's "porch story," told when I was ill in bed, made me understand how difficult it was for my mother to accept herself. Her shame that her family came from a plantation, that her grandmother was a mixed child of rape, still unsettled her. There was no lens to make the past less frightening, less upsetting to her sense of decorum. She wasn't an "Uncle Tom," a "white wannabe," as the '60s lexicon would have termed it. Rather, she was proud of her racial heritage, but her pride was bound up with the etiquette of a white world that was a figment of the '50s. Like Booker T. Washington, Mother thought that if she worked hard enough, adopted the tastes of white middle-class culture, she would be accepted. This desire for acceptance was her weakness, an insidious insecurity, an illogical belief that what she was—a mixed-blood, New World African American—was something to be ashamed of.

I say what she was, was just fine. A special mix of humanity shaped my mother, as it shaped and continues to shape us all. Mother's fears wouldn't let her embrace all the recesses and twists of her blood. Rather, she established categories that contradicted themselves: being black was fine, being a descendent of slaves was not fine. Being lovely like Lena Horne was fine, being descended from a white Master wasn't. If she could have, she would have suppressed half the blood that made her.

Sometimes I dreamt Mother and I were sitting on the bed side by side, reflected in a wardrobe mirror. "See," she'd say to me, "you look just like me." And I would nod, saying, "There's plenty of good ghosts in our blood." "Yes," she'd answer; then, just like a child's (a Native American's?) ritual of bonding, we'd prick our fingers, press them flesh to flesh, blood to blood, swearing, "Always." Swearing our ties couldn't be unbound. But I wake, knowing Mother would have preferred purity. Being mixed-blood was too complicated for her. From either racial side, she thought she was being judged. Never at ease, her behavior became more and more rigid. Friendships, familial relations became a trial.

In the meantime, I tell my children to celebrate rivers. The roar of people, faces, histories stirring in their blood.

My census category is African American. It has always been. Yet this category doesn't deny all the people in my blood, my genes, bubbling beneath my skin. I pass it all on. That's what Grandmother taught me during those years she raised me from a squalling infant to a third grader trying to be in a complicated world.

Everyone is a mixed-blood stew.
Embrace humanity.

Prejudice is sinful—all blood flows red.

"Dream big, Jewell, girl. Educate yourself.
There's things you've got to do."

Did I ever tell you about the time I left school?"

"No, ma'am," I fibbed. Grandmother had told me lots of tales about the importance of "getting ed-u-ca-ted." But I'd never heard this one.

Grandmother looked wistful and sad. "Down South, my folks felt eight grades of schooling was enough. After all, I was pledged to be a clerk's wife. I knew how to cook and clean. I served in the church, passing out fans with portraits of Jesus to folks who cried and shivered with the Holy Spirit. They fell down, felt the Spirit, more times than any Northerner I've met since."

"Even Mrs. Watson?"

"Yes. She'd dead now. Passed last summer."

I felt sorry for it. Just as I felt sorry that Grandmother had grown even older. In eight years, she'd grown to seem ancient.

"My Papa died too. Down South."

I had flashes of an old man sitting on that big white porch, never talking, just basking in Grandmother fussing over him. "More tea?" "A blanket? How 'bout a blanket to keep out the chill?" "Would you like rhubarb pie?" Great-grandfather had been like a skeleton with some skin poured on, but he'd seemed impish, like a child, as his favorite daughter had cared for him.

Grandmother hadn't lived down South for over forty years. Forty years, she'd been away as her Seminole-black grandmother had died, as her mother had died of diabetes, as her father had grown deaf, less hale, less strong.

I'd lived with my mother in California one year shy of the time I'd lived with my grandmother in Pittsburgh. Seven years compared to eight. I preferred my time with my grandmother.

On my sixteenth birthday, Mother kicked me out of her house. The reason she gave was that I'd used butter instead of margarine. Butter was only for her gentlemen guests. Her and

Pop had only lasted for a year. It's still a mystery as to why I'd had to live with my mother. No one would let me go home to Grandmother and Rev. Pop remarried, and while he sheltered me for a year, I was out of place in his home, with a new wife and toddler son. I got a job, saved, graduated high school early, and, at sixteen, bought a plane ticket to Pittsburgh, my only true home.

For the first time in a long time, I was on the porch, talking to the woman I felt was more my mother than my mother. More a parent than either my mother or my father. But it wasn't a summer night. It was winter. Why we went outside to talk, I'll never know. I can only guess that Grandmother had missed the porch moments as much as I had. It didn't matter that the season was all wrong.

We bundled up warmly. I, in my aunt's coat. Our breath barely warmed the cold. Grandmother looked upward at the moon.

"I was supposed to be just the right gal to help uplift the race. But one summer I met a sailor so light he could pass for white. Before I knew it I was up North, a place with race problems too, with two kids and monthly government payroll checks. When those checks stopped coming, I worked as a maid, cleaned floors, toilets, anything to keep my babies fed."

Pittsburgh wasn't so gritty anymore. The steel mills had been pulled down. Rev still sat at the table, only snoring, too tired to go to work, too filled with lung cancer to speak without sounding like sandpaper. He could no longer shout and testify about the Lord. Instead, he mumbled to himself and moaned. He was living longer than anyone expected. I always suspected it was because of Grandmother's love.

I'd grown. My sister, Tonie, stayed with my mother in California. My father stayed West, proudly raising a child to carry the family name—Parker. But still the house on Pittsburgh's north side was filled. My aunt was older, more tired. She'd had a second daughter. Her eldest—my cousin Aleta—was unmarried and pregnant with her first child. The boys were in middle school.

It was too cold to sit. My bones trembled, for I'd gotten used to all-season California sunshine.

The porch wasn't magical, just some steps sprinkled with rock salt to keep us from slipping and falling down. But it was magical standing next to Grandmother.

Pittsburgh was only special in memory. There was a bright shining airport and a high-tech downtown, but where Grandmother and Rev lived, life had turned bleaker and more despairing. More vacant lots, more buildings boarded up with pine flats. More trash and rats scurrying across the street.

To my mind, only Grandmother was special and always would be.

"Read. Read all you can. I don't read well. But I want to."

"Why don't you?"

"Still too much laundry and cooking." She rubbed her aching side, then blew on her gloveless hands. "Go to bed now. We have to get up early in the morning."

"For what?"

"You'll see." She opened the front door, and we stomped off the snow in the vestibule. I opened the second door and headed upstairs.

"Wear clean underwear," Grandmother shouted.

Two flights to bed. Everything seemed smaller, dustier; the rooms more cluttered with junk. Old mementoes: photographs, ancient report cards, a television console that didn't work, clothes outgrown, clothes never worn. The rocking horse was still in the top bedroom. Springs rusty, its paint scratched in a hundred different places, the rocking horse looked more like D. H. Lawrence's rocking demon.

I fell to sleep thinking of porch stories:

"Jewell, child, did I ever tell you about the Africans who could fly?"

In the morning, Grandmother was shaking my shoulder, telling me to get up. "It's time to go."

She was dressed in her good coat. Like the time she took the telephone call telling her that Aunt Hattie was dead. "Hurry up now."

I hurried, washed my face and hands, and dressed. Afterwards, I flew down the steps two at a time, and Grandmother stood by the telephone stand. "Rev's waiting outside."

This was special. Rev, driving as sick as he was, rather than me and Grandmother taking the bus.

We rode through the declining neighborhood. Folks shouted, "Hey, Mrs. Thornton." "How do, Rev?" Grandmother and Rev would nod, wave their hands like royalty. The neighborhood soon blended into Allegheny Park, where I'd bought popcorn and snow cones. Soon, the car was rattling across the bridge spanning the three rivers, into downtown. Rev parked in a high-rise garage (five dollars!), saying, "I'll wait." He had his thermos and the black-owned newspaper, the *Pittsburgh Courier*.

"Where we going?"

"Look at you. You don't have warm clothes on your back."

It was true. I'd flown home to Pittsburgh in the dead of winter with nothing but California clothes. Today, I tugged Aleta's spare jacket close to my throat. But the jacket was made for the fall, with its colored leaves, not for snow and a wind howling off the river.

"Your daddy and your mother should've known better."

I didn't say anything. Just followed Grandmother into the elevator, across the street, and into the spinning doors of Mellon Bank.

The warmth felt good, but the bank wasn't integrated like the banks in California.

"I'd like to see a loan officer," Grandmother said, sounding prim.

"Just a minute. Mrs.?"

"Thornton."

"Do you have an appointment?"

"No." Grandmother's shoulders rounded just a bit.

"Just a minute, Mrs. Thornton." The young woman, blonde, in a red suit, smiled.

A minute became an hour, and Grandmother sat, straight back, eyes fixed ahead. I played with my love beads.

A loan officer, a plain, stern-looking man, came to meet Grandmother. Shook her hand and said, "Follow me." His cubicle wasn't much bigger than a bathroom, but it was impressive, with a wide walnut desk and gold-plated pens and a nameplate that said Jonathan Stevens.

Grandmother folded her hands in her lap. I kept mine stuffed in my pockets.

"I want a loan."

"Do you have collateral?"

"What?"

"Something to guarantee your investment."

Grandmother pushed me forward, though there was no

place to go. "My granddaughter here. Smart. Kind. A good girl. She's going to college."

My jaw dropped. This was the first time I'd heard of it.

"Allegheny Community College. We need midyear tuition and money for warm clothes."

I thought Stevens would laugh and send Grandmother on her way. Instead, he pulled out a sheet and a pen. "How much is tuition?"

"About ninety-eight dollars."

"And books. Don't forget books."

"She has to buy those too?"

"Oh, yes, my daughter did too. At Smith. Cost me a fortune. One hundred for books," he said slowly, timing his words as he wrote it down.

Grandmother relaxed. At ease with being taken seriously.

"And bus fare." She tapped the desk.

"Bus fare."

"And a coat. She doesn't have one."

He looked at me. I squirmed, uncomfortable in Aleta's too-small, too-lightweight jacket. "And mittens. Scarves. Sweaters. Boots."

"A hat?" I asked. My ears were awfully cold.

"A hat." Stevens smiled at me. I didn't shift. Just stood and pulled myself a bit taller, feeling Grandmother proud beside me.

"Five hundred dollars."

Grandmother flinched.

"Five hundred will get her what she needs and pay for *two* semesters at school."

Grandmother smiled, as though this man's faith meant something.

"Collateral?" he asked. Then, almost apologetically, again he asked, "Collateral?"

Grandmother stared at him, then pointed. "She's my collateral."

"I meant anything you own. Like a house. A car? Something to secure the loan."

"She's my collateral. My grandchild here."

Both of us, brown-eyed and wide-eyed, were staring at the blue-eyed man. He was dressed in a fine blue suit. Wool. His small cubicle held prettier furniture than anything in my grandmother's or my mother's or my father's house. He twirled his gold pen.

"How old are you?"

"Sixteen."

"A bit young, aren't you?"

"I graduated high school. Honors, even."

"I brought her diploma." Grandmother unfurled it on his desk as if it were precious.

He barely glanced at the paper. Just kept looking at me. I have no idea what he saw—but as if some light had been turned on, he suddenly grinned. "Terrific collateral, a smart girl."

After a semester at Allegheny Community, I got accepted to Carnegie-Mellon University to study theater and dance.

"You're storytelling," Grandmother said.

And she was right. And so proud. I was the first generation to go to college. Through me, Grandmother had made her education dreams come true.

But that first evening, after we'd gone to Lerner's and bought me a winter coat, after Rev had driven us home, after supper with all the kids demanding, "More pork chops, more beans." More this, more that. We went out to the porch. Me, in my new coat, hat, and scarf. Grandmother held two cups of hot cocoa. There was nothing right about our porch time. It wasn't a summer night. No tale. Just a minute of privacy on the steps.

"How'd you know I wanted to go to college?"

"Because I wanted to. Want to. You'll do what I didn't do.

"Don't feel sorry for me. I'm a different generation. If I could I'd just go South. Imagine, me, on the porch, in the garden, shaping pole beans. I'd be ever so happy. If I can't have books, I'll take the Earth."

She never had either.

It took me a while to understand Grandmother's life. Trapped in Pittsburgh. Without soil to till or time enough to read.

That night, our last time on our porch (but I didn't know it then), I asked, "Why?"

Snowflakes fell. Light fluffs. Puff balls settling on my nose.

"Why? Someone's gotta make sure the children survive. Who else is going to pass stories down?"

In a blink of time, I was seventeen. A freshman. Older, not necessarily wiser. Scholarships and loans were making dreams possible. Grandmother and Rev still sent $46.00 each month to Mellon Bank. Then I was eighteen. Nineteen. And like another blink in time, Grandmother was caring for more of my cousin's children. Babies having babies. Three generations of kids.

I called Grandmother on a Sunday from my college dorm's phone. I said, "I'll visit next week." Grandmother sounded tired but happy. Another Christmas had passed, but winter was still holding on and Good Friday was weeks off.

"In Carolina, I'd be planning my garden. Pole beans, sweet peas, and early tomatoes. I'm too old to be raising kids. One day, down South, I'm going to put my feet up and watch my garden grow."

"Next week, when I see you . . . will you tell me about cauls?"

"Why you want to know about that?"

"Research. I'm writing a novel." A junior, I'd switched my major to English.

"Cauls are special. In Carolina, Mama's midwife would talk about cauls. Meant the baby had the gift, the sight. None of Mama's babies were born with it, but the midwife kept hoping. Midwife said her Mam had told her just what to do with it."

"What's that?"

"I'm not sure I remember. Bury it. Light some candles. Save a piece and boil it with tea. I don't know what all else. Down South, folks can be funny."

"Are you funny?"

Grandmother laughed, and her voice sounded years younger. In my mind's eye, I could see her in the hallway, just beyond the vestibule, sitting in the telephone chair, her arms draped on the small table. Flowery housedress. Pink terry-cloth slippers. Her hair squeezed tight in curlers.

"I was always funny. So were you. Do you remember the time when you thought Aquarius was a sign from God? You were too cute. You asked me for the Bible. 'Specially since I told you it was your sign."

I laughed.

"But it's true, you know. Everything in life is a sign. You are the water-bearer. Carrying tales between this world and the next." She sighed. "Love you. Got to put the kids to bed."

"Love you. See you Friday."

Tuesday, walking from the store with my youngest cousins, Grandmother collapsed onto the sidewalk, clutching at her heart. I imagine the boys jumping up and down, waving, hollering for help.

This is the tale I was told:

"A kind man stopped his car and offered a ride to the hospital. Ernestine was still conscious. She asked for Mercy. Mercy Hospital.

"When they got to Mercy, the nurses made her wait. Ernestine was having trouble breathing. The eldest boy answered questions: 'Yes, she has pressure problems. Diabetes. Pains in her chest.'

"Ernestine was taken upstairs for heart monitoring. They rolled her wheelchair into the elevator. By the time they got to the right floor, Ernestine was dead."

I was dazed, shaken, guilty that I hadn't seen Grandmother. Hadn't said a proper good-bye. Later, our family doctor said, "They should've taken Ernestine to Allegheny. Poor Mercy only had one heart monitor and cardiac machine. That's why they took the elevator—they were taking her to it. Allegheny, a rich county hospital, would've had a machine in Emergency. Would've been able to save her right then and there."

I don't know if that's true. I don't know if Grandmother's heart could have been saved.

At the funeral, all her many children cried.

I have been to Carolina. I stayed in a porchless, modern hotel and stared out the windows on the twenty-first floor looking at a skyline of concrete, steel, and a light blue sky. Clouds drifted west to further horizons I could only dream about.

I did not rent a car. I did not visit the ancestral home. I was afraid Grandmother's home would be a will-o'-the-wisp, a mirage cloaked by humid heat. I was afraid the soil that had nurtured Grandmother's love would appear only barren and dry like a desert to me.

Older now, I understand better the complex weave of how generations of children chained Grandmother like steel. I understand, too, that Grandmother would not, could not, have behaved any other way. She would mother us all as long as she believed we needed her. I know I needed her. I need her still.

The dead are with us.

I speak with Grandmother nearly every night. And I hear echoing through time, through memory, her stories, sayings, and her "wisdoms." I conjure her loving hands, her big-hearted smile, and generosity. I try to "live right" because that is how a Southern gal raised down South in Carolina raised me.

I tell stories. Write stories down. That is the legacy Grandmother gave me. "Pass it all down, Jewell, girl. You never know when a story you tell is the one special story someone needs to hear. Stories. You tell them, Jewell, girl."

I do. I will.

Porch stories. Life stories. Grandmother's wisdom and tales.

* *Remember your name. Who-you-be.*
  Be in love with your good self.

* *Wear clean underwear.*
  Don't let anyone ever think there's trash in you.

* *Never underestimate the power of feelings.*
  Being well-loved means good memories.

* *A piece of string can be more precious than a rope of pearls.*

* *You never need an excuse for joy.*
  Celebrate being alive.

* *When your soul aches, speak to the dead.*
  Ancestors who loved you, still do. They're always listening.
  If you let yourself hear, they'll guide you.

* *Love yourself despite and because of your flaws.*
  Strive to be better.
  Every woman is your sister.
  Celebrate a woman's power for creation.

* *Everyone is a mixed-blood stew.*
  Embrace humanity.

* *Prejudice is sinful—all blood flows red.*

* *Dream big. Educate yourself.*
  Live purposefully—there are things in this world you are
  meant to do.

* *Life isn't all about you, what you take.*
  It's about sharing a loving legacy with your family.
  Give, and your heart and soul will be enriched.

* *Share your own porch stories.*
  Pass your wisdom and heritage down . . . across the
  generations.

Grandmothers are truly special. With luck, we all will become grandmothers; if not to our children's children, then to our neighborhoods' children.

I have tried to live my life according to my grandmother's tales. My secret shame (and now no longer a secret) is that one fall day, when I was a sophomore in college, I went riding my new ten-speed bicycle in some worn-out clothes. I was flying downhill, and a police car rolled out of a parking lot. I braked and flew over my bike's rails. The policemen never got out of their car . . . maybe they weren't too interested in me (bike riding wasn't a crime), or maybe it was because they saw me get up and mount my bike. I registered that they were white; to this day, I have no idea whether skin color played any part in their decision to stay in the car.

After a few spins of the wheel, I slid off my bike, limping and trying to hold the bike steady. A car slowed. I thought it was the policemen, but it was a middle-aged man, angling to the right, past the steering wheel, asking, "Are you alright? Do you need a ride?"

I shook my head no. Though I knew I was hurt, I was afraid of being kidnapped.

The car kept following me; I grew paler, more in pain.

"Let me help you." A warm, brown man got out of the car. Put my flaming red bike in his trunk and helped me, wincing, into the car. He took me to Allegheny Hospital. Emergency.

I said, "Thank you," not knowing then that I'd broken my collarbone and two ribs. Just before I fainted, I had a vision of Grandmother scolding me.

I'd put on clean underwear, but my underwear had holes, and I knew that as far as Grandmother was concerned, it wouldn't count.

It would not be wrong to say that Grandmother saved my life. Her tales dominated. With each decade, I'd understand more and more of what her stories meant.

Grandmother's guidance is everlasting. More than anyone, she taught me how to live. She taught me how to nurture myself, and my children, with words.

Like a magician or conjure woman, she turned all spaces into womanist spaces. The kitchen table, the garden, the porch, a child's bedroom, the living room, even the basement with its coal furnace and damp laundry were all spaces where Grandmother taught values as effortlessly as she breathed. Wherever Grandmother reigned, there was spiritual uplift and healing.

Handing me my grits, she'd talk about making a good start to each and every day. "Jewell, child, new day. New opportunities. New you."

I loved when she combed my hair, layering grease on my dry scalp. I felt safe, cared for . . . groomed in a deeply primeval, deeply special way. "You are beautiful, Jewell, girl."

I loved when she let me help her snip a rose from her Blanche Mallerin. To this day, I love flowers . . . any and all kinds. I watched Grandmother lavish care over her two rose bushes that had a barely enough rocky ground to grow in, coal flecks that sucked out air and dirtied their fulsome beauty, and no chance for a butterfly or bee to admire their beauty in our too-urban world. Yet each time we snipped one of the few precious blooms, Grandmother would say, "Thank you kindly," and we'd bring it inside to sit in a glass on the kitchen sill. Cooking pork chops, washing dishes, relaxing over a cup of tea, I'd see Grandmother's eyes gaze at the lonely bloom and she'd smile. When the yellow rose died, she carry it back to her tiny yard and bury it between the two rose bushes. "Thank you kindly," she'd say again.

Grandmother was teaching me about nature's beauty and its capacity to nourish our souls. She was also teaching me the patience to admire growing things and participate in their glory by watering, adding fertilizer, pinching back dead leaves, and accepting Mother Nature's gift of a rose.

But of all the spaces where Grandmother reigned supreme, porches—our front steps—were her favorite. Why?

Clearly, the porch was part of her childhood memories and recalled a time when she and her people were tied to the land and used the porch to socialize, admire crops and gardens, and to escape confining indoor heat. Grandmother was following a long-ingrained pattern of porch talk even though her view was of a street filled with parked and speeding cars and houses that made up a brick, tenement ghetto.

Outdoors, though, Grandmother was connected to her community. Outdoors, Grandmother's spirit was liberated from household chores.

The magic, the transformation that took place on steps, stoops, and porches was special. These are the spaces that connect inside to outside, home to community, the private to the public self, the less mobile elders to the highly mobile youth. These are the spaces that are created by humankind's efforts that are still open to God's sky.

When I look at the paintings of African American artists, I invariably see porches, stoops, steps, and a hive of socializing. Men, but especially women, telling stories to the next generation. Oral storytelling is central to African American tradition. Slaves forged community, cherished wisdoms and traditions by gathering together to speak and to listen. Grandmother told the story of slaves becoming birds and flying off to freedom. When I was an adult, I discovered that Grandmother's story was a nineteenth-century folktale. In Julius Lester's *Black Folktales* and Virginia Hamilton's *The People Who Could Fly*, there are retellings of slaves outwitting the Master, trumping injustice, and flying off to freedom. Lester's and Hamilton's retellings come from the millions of elders like my grandmother, who passed the oral tale down through the generations before it became written down.

Oral storytelling is central to all of humanity. The voice telling the tale extends to the ancient *griots* of Africa as well as to Western culture's Homer. In truth, mostly all surviving twentieth-first–century cultures have moved from oral to written literary traditions.

While I've told my children my grandmother tales, this written narrative allows me to share them with you, dear reader, and for us together, as writer and reader, to make a connection about the wonder of being human. You may be older, younger, of a different cultural and ethnic group, from another country or another tribe. Not yet a grandmother or a grandmother ten times over. Even a great-grandmother. None of these differences should matter. What matters is capturing a human voice, a story, and *sharing* one human to another. If you can feel, see, be moved by my grandmother's words, then you and I, dear reader, have made our own porch together. *In this space. On these pages. In this book. And in, each other's hearts. We are kin.*

What is the appeal of the porch? Whether it is a southern veranda, a beachfront porch, a balcony with a chair, or an impoverished set of steps, *porch* is a state of being. A reaffirmation that life is good—that time taken for rest, for enjoying nature, family, and community are all good. Telling tales, sharing porch stories, is all about love.

I am wiser and stronger because of the porch, the steps, the stoop, because of a black woman who sought no one's permission to be—but just lived—struggling with grace while sharing bountiful love.

In the back of this book are pages for you to write down your grandmother's porch stories. It doesn't matter if your grandmother—whether she be kin, a friend, or some elder from your community—told the tales on the porch, from a wheelchair, or cooking and perspiring over a hot stove. If your grandmother is dead, the key is to remember and write down her tales for posterity. If your grandmother is still alive, ask her to fill these pages. Or if she prefers, celebrate her by listening to her tales and writing them down for her. Prose on a page is another kind of love.

If you are a grandmother, an elder who has stories to share, here is a space for you to begin. Just imagine you're sitting on a porch telling a story to a child, a daughter, a friend, a neighbor that you love and who loves you. The words will come.

In fairy tales, cultural stories, older women are often cast as crones. The image is one of a negative witch. An evildoer, a malingerer—disgraced, dissatisfied with old age.

I prefer to believe that older women bear gifts to pass on from one woman to the next. Older women aren't perfect. They aren't always wise. But they have empowering tales of their own life's journey and can empower others. An older woman—a grandmother—is like any other woman, still trying to fulfill the promise of her life's journey. Life isn't over until it's over. Learning never stops.

Encourage memories to flow . . . whether your grandmother is alive or whether you're conjuring her in memory, write down a story your grandmother told you and ask yourself, "Why did she tell this tale?" What lesson was she teaching? What value was she passing down? And if both your grandmothers are dead, talk with an elder, a wise woman from your community.

All of us have stories to tell.

It doesn't matter where the story is told, only that you hear it, write it down, learn from it, and share it.

You tell them, Jewell, child.

"I did, Grandmother. I did. Just like you told me."

I am listening. All of us are listening.

Jewell, child, yes.

Just like you, Grandmother. We are all telling our tales.

My Porch Stories